• Basic Instructions and Special Tips •

Look these ideas over before you travel *Back In Time* to your first project.
Have a safe journey!

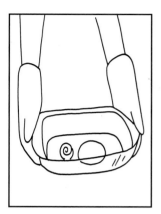

1. Knead clay until soft to make it easy to work with. Cover working surfaces with wax paper, then clean surfaces and wash your hands thoroughly. Bake clay on an ovenproof dish in a 275° oven. Do not use a Microwave.

5. When painting or working with messy materials, don't forget to protect your work surface with plastic or newspaper and your clothes with an apron or old shirt. Keep a roll of paper towels handy to wipe up spills.

2. IMPORTANT! When you see the 'helping hand' symbol on a project page, it means you may need adult supervision to do the project. Always use care when using tools or a heat source. Be careful and safe!

Waxed Paper

6. To make sure paint doesn't seep through the shirts or fabric, use a piece of cardboard or wax paper inside the shirt or under fabric while painting. Tape the sleeves and excess shirt together at the back of the board.

3. Trace the patterns as needed onto the tracing paper. Lay the traced pattern on top of project surface. Place transfer, or graphite paper under the pattern then trace over design with a soft pencil, or crayon.

7. There are some basic supplies that are used throughout the book which are not always in the project supply list. Some of these general supplies are: paper clips, toothpicks, paper, tracing paper etc.

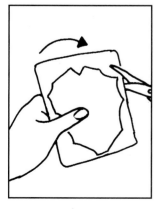

4. When cutting with a pair of scissors, always work slowly and evenly. Hold the material you are cutting with the opposite hand, turning it toward the scissors as you cut.

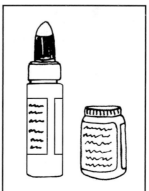

8. For best results, always read and follow directions given on each product label. Some products may seem to do the same thing, but there may be important differences you need to know.

• TABLE OF CONTENTS •

Cobra Pen Topper
by Dimples Mucherino

The Asp, or Egyptian Cobra is the smallest and most common type of cobra. Cobras were often used as a subject for jewelry and decorative items in ancient Egypt.

You will need:
1" Ball white clay
Acrylic paint - ivory & black
Satin glaze

Pencil (preferably with no eraser)
Paintbrushes
Ruler

1. Knead clay till soft and smooth. Roll on flat surface into a 12" long rope leaving one end (the head) $1/2$" wide. Taper the other end (the tail) to form a point.

2. Rest head on side of pencil then wrap body around pencil several times, ending with tail folded back and forth in an "S" along same side as head. Bake on an oven proof glass surface at 275°F for 15 minutes per $1/4$" of thickness, with good ventilation. DO NOT USE MICROWAVE OVEN. Avoid over baking. Thicker pieces may require additional baking time. Let cool, then remove the pencil.

3. Apply ivory paint to snake. Dip tips of brush in black paint. Blot on paper towels. Dab brush randomly along head and body. Dot eyes and nostrils black with end of paintbrush. Let dry. Coat with glaze.

Option: Substitute eraser clay instead of regular clay to make a snake that will devour all your mistakes!

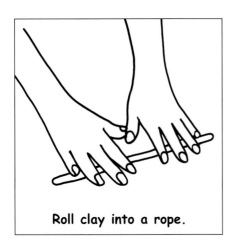

Roll clay into a rope.

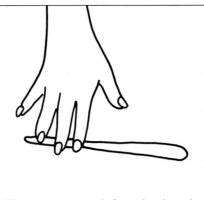

Flatten one end for the head.

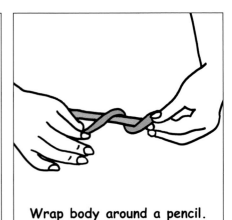

Wrap body around a pencil.

Polyform Original Sculpey® Polymer Clay, Glaze; Delta Ceramcoat® Acrylic Paint; Fiskars® Ruler

Potpourri Mummy

by Patty Cox

Egypt is known for its pyramids, the final resting place for those that have died, and also for its means of preserving bodies as mummies. The body was wrapped in strips of cloth and anointed with various oils and scents.

You will need:
2 oz Package white clay
Teaspoon cinnamon
3 Drops cinnamon oil
Mini craft stick
Plastic fork
Pencil

1. Knead cinnamon and 1 drop of oil into the clay.

2. Roll a 3/4" ball for mummy head. Pinch clay to form the nose. Flatten bottom of the nose with a craft stick.

3. Roll a 1/2" ball of clay then roll into a 2" long snake for arms. Roll remaining clay into a log, about 3" long. Roll one end slightly smaller than the other. Fold smaller end upward. Stand log on its folded feet. Press the craft stick in clay to separate feet.

4. Score head bottom and shoulder top with plastic fork. Press head onto shoulders. Score arms and body with fork, then press the arms in position on the body.

5. Make wrap impression around body using a mini craft stick. Press a sharpened pencil into the top of head to form a well.

6. Bake on an oven proof glass surface at 275°F for 15 minutes per 1/4" of thickness, with good ventilation. **DO NOT USE A MICROWAVE OVEN**. Avoid over baking. Thicker pieces may require additional baking time. Let cool then add 2 drops of cinnamon oil in top of head.

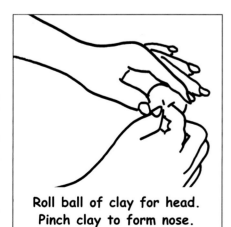

Roll ball of clay for head. Pinch clay to form nose.

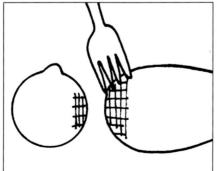

Score bottom of head and top of shoulder with fork.

Press pencil point into top of head to form a well.

Polyform Original Sculpey® Polymer Clay; Darice® Mini Craft Stick

Hieroglyphics
by Kathi Taylor Shearer

Hieroglyphics is a form of picture writing. Small pictures were used to represent words, actions or ideas. There were over 700 letters, but no vowels.

You will need:

for each Letter
4 $\frac{1}{2}$" x 6" Corrugated cardboard
4 $\frac{1}{2}$" x 6" Burlap
4 $\frac{1}{2}$" x 6" Recycled paper
Adhesive backed foam - any color
Black permanent marker
Plain brayer and roller handle
Black ink pad

for Book
Two 4 $\frac{1}{2}$" x 6" pieces card stock - any color
Paper trimmer
$\frac{1}{8}$" Hole punch
Metallic gel pens
9" Length black jute
Glue
Scissors
Ruler

1. Make one hieroglyphic alphabet letter page by gluing the burlap to cardboard for letter block. Draw hieroglyphic and alphabet letter on foam sheet with black marker, then cut out. Peel backing from foam, then press onto the burlap.

2. To print, lay recycled paper on top of letter block. Roll brayer in black ink pad then over paper. Experiment first with the amount of dye on the roller and amount of pressure needed when printing.

3. Repeat steps 1 and 2 for additional pages for your hieroglyphic book, or each person can make one letter for a group print.

4. Use gel pens and the two pieces of card stock to design your own hieroglyphic book cover. You could design your name, for example.

5. Punch holes in the 4 $\frac{1}{2}$" x 6" piece of white paper to act as your guide to punching the holes on each printed page and in the front and back book covers. Arrange printed pages in alphabetical order between the front and back covers, aligning the holes.

6. Thread the jute through the holes from the front, then double knot in back to secure.

Press letters onto burlap.

Lay paper on top of letters.
Roll inked brayer over paper.

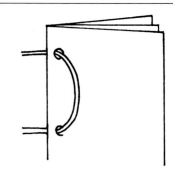

Thread jute through holes.
Tie in back to secure.

Hieroglyphic Alphabet

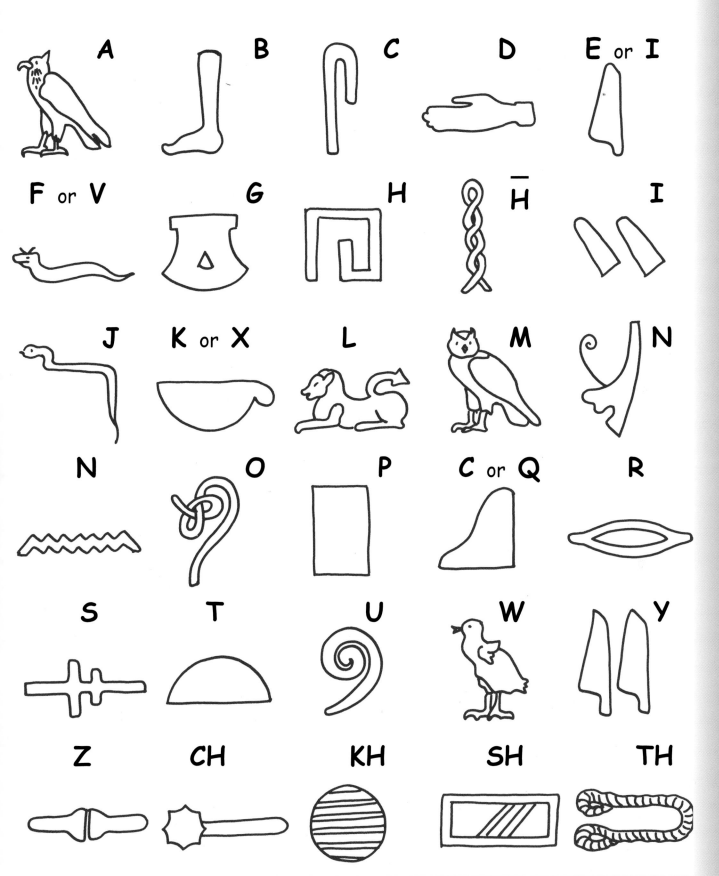

A   B   C   D   E or I

F or V   G   H   H̄   I

J   K or X   L   M   N

N   O   P   C or Q   R

S   T   U   W   Y

Z   CH   KH   SH   TH

Strathmore Craft Paper, Brite Hue Paper; Darice® Foamies™, Jute;
Fiskars® Paper Trimmer, Scissors, Ruler, Hand Punch

Collar and Cuffs
by Beth Wheeler

Jewelry was an important part of the dress in ancient Egypt. The nobility in particular, adorned themselves with beautiful symmetrical collars of metal and precious stones, and beautiful bangles and cuffs.

You will need:
Empty cereal box or cardboard
3 Sheets gold plastic backed
  foil sheets
24 Gauge wire
Assorted acrylic gem stones
Jewelry glue
Contact adhesive
1/2" Wide double stick tape
Scissors
Craft Snips
1/8" Hole punch
Round elastic

1. Cut cereal box into flat sheets. Place pattern on plain side of cardboard. Trace and cut out two collar pieces and four cuff pieces.

2. Place cardboard pieces on wrong side of foil sheets. Trace and cut out each one 1/2" larger than the pattern all the way around.

3. Wrap foil around cardboard pieces, securing wrap around portion to cardboard with double stick tape.

4. Trace and cut out each piece on another sheet of foil, this time the exact size of the cardboard piece. Secure on opposite side of cardboard piece with double stick tape. This should cover cardboard completely.

5. Punch holes as indicated on patterns through all layers. Join two cuff pieces by inserting elastic through holes and tying in a knot. Cut elastic to fit your wrists comfortably.

6. Join collar pieces with elastic. Cut piece of elastic large enough to fit comfortably around your neck. Insert ends through punched holes, and knot in back.

7. Using craft snips, cut and bend wire as shown on pattern. Make three for each cuff and five for the collar piece.

8. Glue wire pieces on the outer edges of collar and cuffs.

9. Glue acrylic gem stones in place along inner edge of collar and cuffs.

Reynolds® Bright Ideas™ Ultra™ Foil Sheets, Double Sided Tape; Toner Plastics, Inc.™ Fun Wire™; Darice® Acrylic Rhinestones; Fiskars® Scissors, Hole Punch; Beacon Gem-Tac™

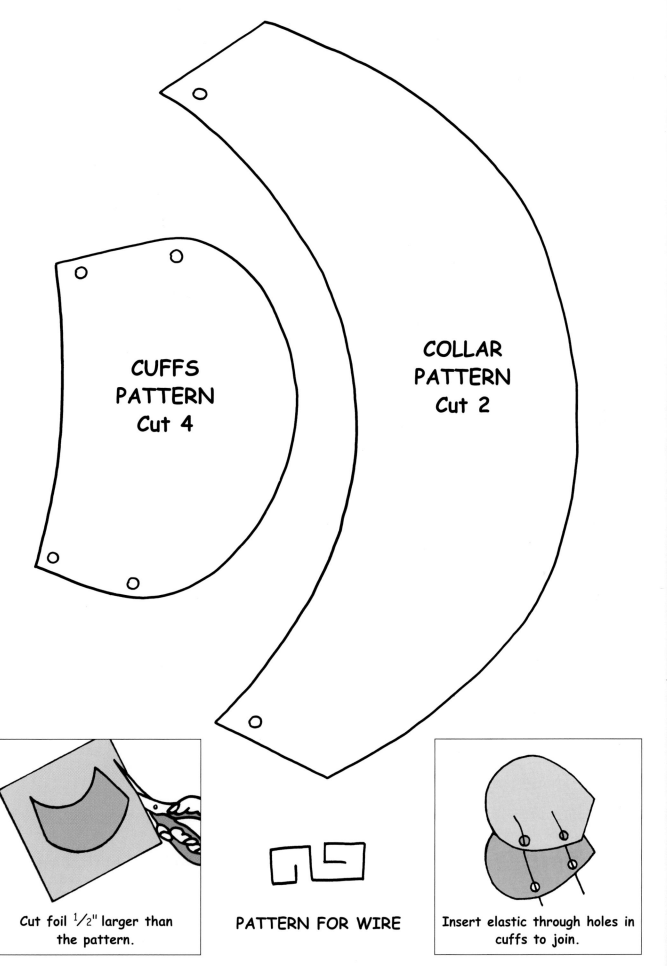

CUFFS
PATTERN
Cut 4

COLLAR
PATTERN
Cut 2

Cut foil 1/2" larger than the pattern.

PATTERN FOR WIRE

Insert elastic through holes in cuffs to join.

Papyrus Fan
by Patty Cox

The word "paper" is derived from the word papyrus. Papyrus is a triangular reed that grows along the bank of the Nile. Egyptians cut the reeds and laid them side by side. Then a second layer was placed over the top at right angles. This was then placed between fabric and pressed between stones for about 6 days.

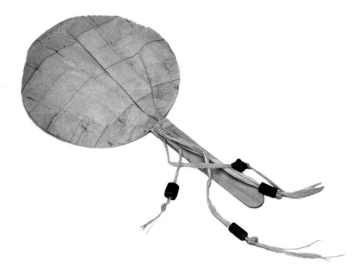

You will need:
2 Coffee filters
Jumbo colored craft stick
Raffia
Assorted Beads
Glue
Mixing cup or jar
Bag Celestial Seasonings black cherry tea
Cup of hot water
Teaspoon of mustard

1. To make the dye, remove tea from bag. Mix tea, water and mustard in cup or jar then set aside. The longer the tea is left to steep, the more pink the dye becomes.

2. Make ¾" to 1" wide accordion folds in back of 2 coffee filters.

3. Soak folded coffee filters in cup of dye 5 to 10 minutes.

4. Remove folded filters from cup and squeeze strips between fingers to remove excess water. Open and let dry.

5. Glue two opened filters together matching folds.

6. Glue and fold the filters around jumbo craft stick as shown.

7. Wrap folded end with raffia. Tie raffia. Thread beads onto raffia, then knot ends to secure beads.

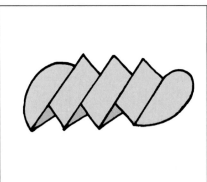

Make accordion folds in back of coffee filters.

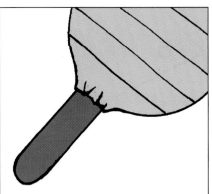

Glue around jumbo craft stick.

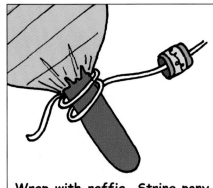

Wrap with raffia. String pony beads on ends.

Darice® Jumbo Craft Stick, Raffia, Beads; Beacon™ Kids Choice Glue™

Egyptian Print
by Sarah Stull

All Egyptian art has the same style and special rules. One of these rules is called "frontalism". This is where the head is always shown in profile, but the body is seen from the front. This print utilizes this design.

You will need:
Sketch paper
Construction paper
Pencil
Pen
Thin styrofoam tray (meat tray)
Acrylic paint - any color
Brayer
Tape

1. Draw Egyptian symbols as shown or create your own on sketch paper. The pattern should be symmetrical (same on one side of the paper as the other). Remember Egyptian faces are in profile.

2. Lay the paper on top of foam tray and tape edges down.

3. Using a pencil, press over drawing to make dent on foam. Remove paper.

4. Trace over pattern on tray with pen.

5. Squeeze paint on a plate and roll brayer through paint. Roll the brayer over the pattern, applying an even coat of paint.

6. Lay construction paper over the paint covered tray and press. Peel off paper to see print. Let dry.

7. You can use the foam tray over again if you'd like to change colors of your print. Just rinse the foam tray and repeat steps 5 and 6.

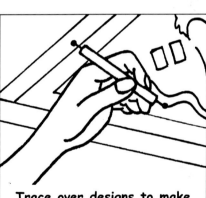

Trace over designs to make impression on tray.

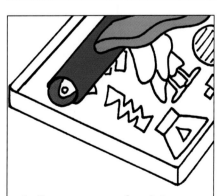

Roll even coat of paint over pattern with a brayer.

EGYPTIAN SYMBOLS

Strathmore Kids™ Series Drawing paper, Construction paper; Fiskars® Brayer

GODDESS PATTERN

DIE CUT DESIGNS ©
AND ® OF ELLISON®

Greek Pots
by Mary Ayres

Many different styles of ceramic pots were used in Ancient Greece. From storage to drinking, they were decorated in many different colors with unique designs. The amphora shape is the traditional tall, handled pot and the klix is a wider bowl-shaped pot with a pedestal.

You will need:
8 1/2" x 11" Metallic gold corrugated paper
Construction paper - black, white
Die cut machine and die
  or pattern and scissors
Small frozen juice can - empty and clean
Decorative corner edgers
Decorative edge scissors
Diamond hand punch
Glue
Ruler

1. Measure and mark 6" from short end of gold ridged paper on back side. Cut along pencil line with decorative edge scissors. Glue gold ridged paper around juice can, overlapping edges in back. Ridges should be running vertically, and bottom edge of paper should be even with the bottom edge of the can. You can make 2 pots from 1 sheet of gold ridged paper.

2. Measure and cut two 3/8" x 9 1/2" strips from black construction paper with decorative edge scissors. Measure and punch diamond shapes, 3/8" apart across black strips.

3. Measure and cut two 1/2" x 9 1/2" strips from white paper with scissors. Glue black strips on top of white strips. Glue assembled strips around top and bottom of pot, overlapping ends in back.

4. Measure and cut a 2 3/4" x 3 3/4" rectangle from white paper. Cut corners of rectangle with corner edgers. Glue rectangle shape vertically to center front of the pot.

5. Using die cut machine and die, or pattern and scissors, cut goddess from black paper. Glue the goddess to white rectangle shape.

Strathmore Kids™ Series Construction Paper, Corduroy Paper; Ellison® XL Ellison® Letter Machine™, Instructional and Decorative Dies; Fiskars® Corner Edgers, Paper Edgers, Scissors, Ruler

Olive Wreath

by Dimples Mucherino

Olive wreaths were a prize in the original Olympics. The first Olympic games were held in 776 B.C.

You will need:
8 1/2" x 12" Plastic backed foil
  sheets - 2 gold, 1 blue
24 Large wood teardrops (1 1/2")
54" Length 18 gauge gold craft wire
Twenty-four, 4" lengths 22 gauge
  gold craft wire
Glue
Scissors
Pencil
Ruler
Craft snips

LEAF PATTERN

1. Form a loop at one end of a 54" length of wire. Loop should be about 6 to 6 1/2" diameter, large enough to fit on top of your head . Form a second loop the same size. Wrap remaining wire around both loops.

2. Wrap one 4" wire tightly onto the wire loops, leaving 1 1/2" for a stem. Attach a second stem facing the same direction about 3/4" behind the first stem. Attach remaining stems around entire base in the same manner.

3. Using large teardrop as a pattern, cut 24 teardrop shapes from blue foil. Outline large teardrop on gold foil adding 1/2 " around the edge to make larger. Cut out 24.

4. Center large wood teardrop on wrong side of gold foil teardrop. Fold and press edges of foil leaves to back of teardrop. Emboss the leaf design on gold foiled side with pencil.

5. With wrong side down, glue the blue foil teardrop to the back sandwiching the 1" wire stem between the foil and teardrop. Continue adding all 24 leaves.

Form wire loops then wrap with wire.

Wrap 4" pieces of wire onto wire loop.

Glue wire stem between between foil and teardrop.

Reynolds® Bright Ideas™ Ultra™ Foil Sheets; Forster® Woodsies™; Toner Plastics, Inc.™ Fun Wire™; Beacon™ Kids Choice Glue™; Fiskars® Scissors, Ruler & Softouch Craft Snips

Tragedy Comedy Mask

by Beth Wheeler

These masks are the symbol for theater and represent masks worn during the Golden Age around 500-300 B.C. This was the first time that theater, as we know it, was written and performed. All actors were male and they all played many different roles, so they wore masks to show their different characters or moods.

You will need:

Two 8" x 10" pieces cardboard
Plastic backed foil sheets - 1 black, 1 gold
Assorted acrylic gem stones
Assorted beads
Two 24" lengths of 24 gauge wire
Stylus
Double stick tape
Scissors
2 Paper clips
Jewelry glue
Pencil

1. Place mask pattern on cardboard. Trace and cut two masks. Trace and cut 2 noses, 4 eyes (reverse pattern for two eyes), and 2 mouths.

2. Place one cardboard mask on the wrong side of black foil and one on gold foil. Trace around each with stylus. Cut each piece out about 1/2" larger than pattern all the way around.

3. Wrap foil around masks, securing cut edges to wrong sides with double sided tape.

4. Trace one nose on gold foil and one on black. Trace two eyes on gold foil (reversing one) and two on black foil (reversing one). Trace one mouth on gold foil and one on black. Cut foil larger than the traced lines all around.

5. Wrap foil around cardboard pieces, securing edges to the back with double sided tape.

6. Place gold eyes, nose, and mouth on black mask. Place black eyes, nose, and mouth on gold mask. Attach with double stick tape, making one mask happy and one sad.

7. Glue acrylic gem stones along top of mask with jewelry glue. Let dry.

8. Bend a spiral in one end of a 24" length of wire to prevent beads from slipping off. Slip beads on piece of wire, distributing beads evenly along length of wire. Bend a spiral in the other end of the wire. Wrap wire and beads around the pencil to curl the wire.

9. Position the wire coil along the top of one of the masks and bend spiral ends to back. Secure spiral in place with glue.

10. Bend paper clip slightly. Glue one edge to top back of mask and use the other paper clip loop as a hanger.

11. Repeat steps 8, 9, and 10 with remaining mask and supplies.

Reynolds® Bright Ideas™ Ultra™ Foil Sheets, Stylus, Double Sided Tape; Darice® Acrylic Beads, Acrylic Rhinestones; Toner Plastics, Inc.™ Fun Wire™; Beacon Gem-Tac™; Fiskars® Scissors

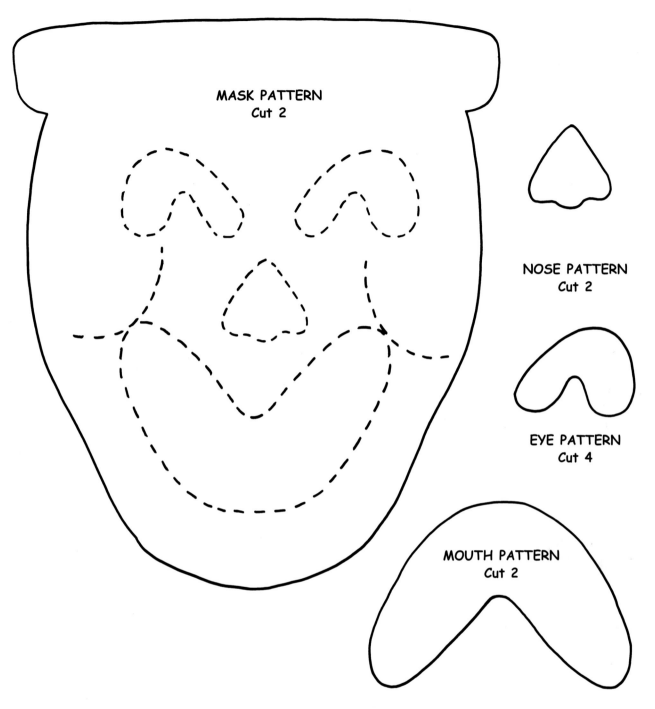

MASK PATTERN
Cut 2

NOSE PATTERN
Cut 2

EYE PATTERN
Cut 4

MOUTH PATTERN
Cut 2

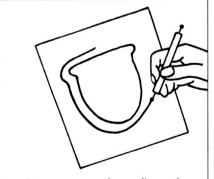

Trace around cardboard template with a stylus.

Wrap extra foil to back of card. Secure with tape.

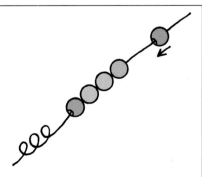

Bend wire into a spiral at each end to secure beads.

Archimedes and Mathematical Solids
by Sandi Genovese

Archimedes lived from 287-212 B.C. Born in Sicily and educated in Egypt, he was the most well-known Greek mathematician. He is known for his study of shapes.

You will need:
Die-cut machine and dies
  or pattern and scissors
Pyramid #1 with Square Base die
Construction Paper: Yellow, Orange,
  Red, Blue, Purple and Green
Tape - clear and double stick

1. Using die cut machine and dies, or pattern and scissors, cut 4 pyramids out of each of the six colors. There will be a total of 24.

2. Fold each one inward on the perforations to assemble. Secure tabs with double stick tape. For heavy usage, tape all the outside edges securely with a strong clear tape.

3. Create 8 pods of 3 pyramids each with top tips together. Make 4 pods from orange, yellow and red, and 4 from blue, purple and green. Reinforce all the seams. Mirroring the colors creates nice patterns, but is not necessary.

4. Arrange the pods in two groups of four with the square pyramid bases flat on the table and flat around the four edges. Tape the two opposite sides on each group of four. Tape the same edge of their opposite side. These are the first four connections.

5. Turn the pyramids over so their bases are on top and flat around the four edges. There are still two groups of four pods. Tape the two pods together as shown on both groups of four. Turn and tape the inside of these edges to strengthen the hinges. These are the fifth and sixth connections.

6. Turn over again with the bases down and tape the two groups together where the two sections come together as shown. Turn and tape the inside of these edges. These are the seventh and eighth connections. The completed project will be secured in eight places .

7. The completed project can be flipped into many configurations including a cube, a rectangle and a stellated rhombic dodecahedron. For heavy use, apply two strips of tape to each side of the eight hinges.

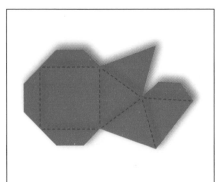
Fold inward on all perforated lines.

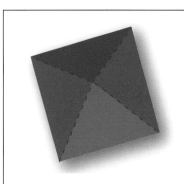
Secure tabs with double stick tape.

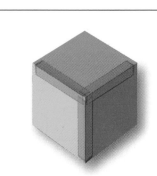
Tape 3 pyramids together to make a pod.

Ellison® XL Ellison® Letter Machine™, Instructional and Decorative Dies; Strathmore Construction Paper

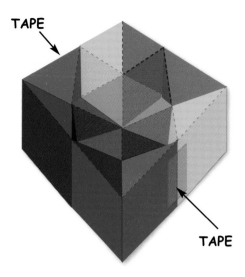

TAPE

TAPE

Tape the two opposite sides on each group
of four

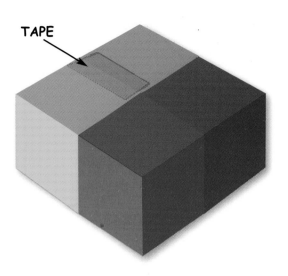

TAPE

Tape 2 groups together on the bottom

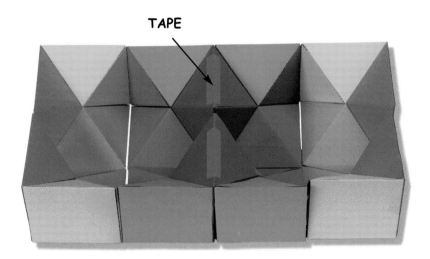

TAPE

Tape inside edges to reinforce the hinge.

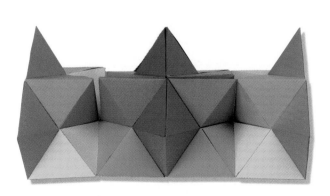

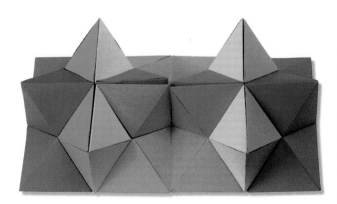

The completed project can be tipped into many configurations.

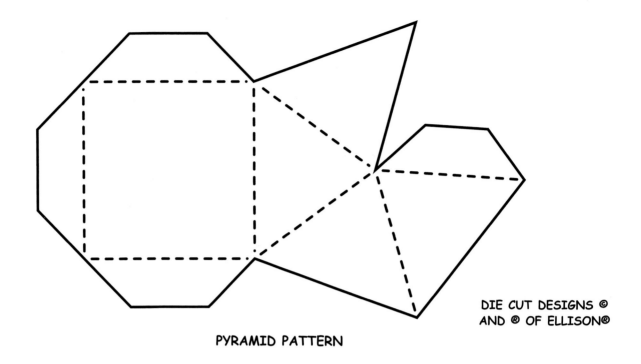

PYRAMID PATTERN

DIE CUT DESIGNS ©
AND ® OF ELLISON®

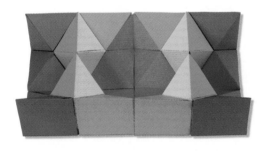

RECTANGLE

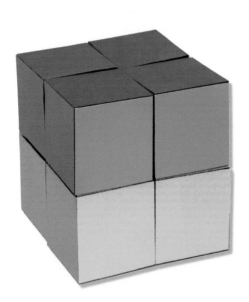

CUBE

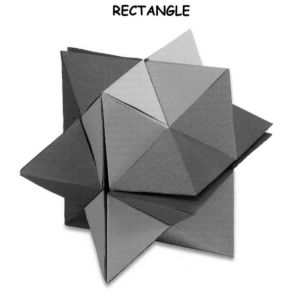

STELLATED RHOMBIC DODECAHEDRON

Column Chalkboard

by Mary Ayres

Doric, Ionic, and Corinthian columns were the most common styles of architectural columns used in Ancient Greece. Doric are the plainest and have no base. Ionic have a circular base and a shallow top with scrolls and Corinthian are the most elaborate with a carved leaf design at the top.

You will need:
5 ¾" x 7 ¾" Chalkboard
  with wood frame
Acrylic paint - white
4 Craft sticks
2 Jumbo craft sticks
2 Mini craft sticks
Flat wood shapes - 2 medium squares,
  4 medium circles
Fine tip black permanent marker
Glue

Meet Caesar and Marc Antony at the forum in March!

1. Paint chalkboard frame, all craft sticks, wood squares and circles white. Let dry.

2. Using black marker, draw a line around the inside of the chalkboard frame and around each of the other wood pieces close to the edges. Draw three lines, vertically down the center of the jumbo craft sticks for the column details. Draw a spiral on two of the wood circles beginning on the outside, working in toward the center. Then on the two remaining circles, repeat the spiral going in the opposite direction.

3. Glue 2 craft sticks side by side centered on the bottom of the chalkboard for steps. Glue the squares to the chalkboard frame on both sides of the steps for the column bases.

4. Glue the jumbo craft stick columns to the side of the chalkboard frame centered above the square bases. Glue the 2 remaining craft sticks angled at the top of chalkboard frame with the ends glued together at the center top for the roof.

5. Glue mini craft sticks angled to the top of the chalkboard frame under the craft sticks with the ends glued together at the center. Glue 2 circles at the top of each column with the spirals going in opposite directions.

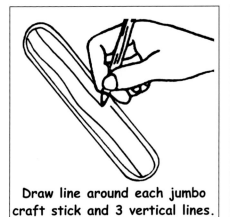

Draw line around each jumbo craft stick and 3 vertical lines.

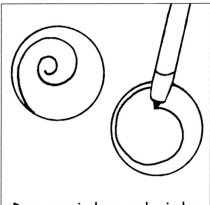

Draw a spiral on each circle.

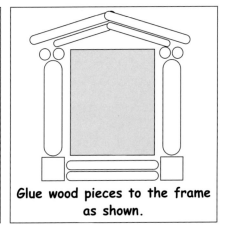

Glue wood pieces to the frame as shown.

Darice® Chalkboard; Forster® Woodsies™, Craft Sticks; Delta Ceramcoat® Acrylic Paint; Beacon™ Kids Choice Glue™

Mosaic Frame
by Cheryl Ball

Originating in Greece, the Romans became famous for their mosaics. Bits of glass and stone were arranged to form designs for jewelry, vases and other art forms.

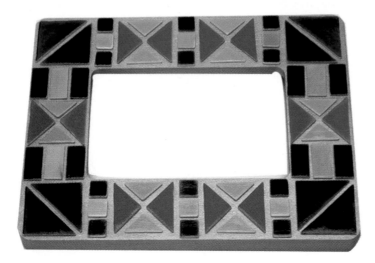

You will need:
Stained glass paint - yellow, orange, pink, purple, blue and green
Gold acrylic paint
All purpose sealer
Flat wood frame (sample 8" x 10")
Assorted wood shapes
Glue
Cardboard
Double stick tape
Scissors
Flat paintbrush
Sanding block

1. Apply a coat of sealer to the frame. Let dry, then sand smooth. Paint the frame with two coats of the gold acrylic paint. Let dry between coats. Set aside.

2. Arrange wood shapes on frame in the desired pattern, or refer to photo for placement. Do not glue.

3. Press strips of double stick tape onto the cardboard. Press wood shapes onto the tape in the design from the frame. This will make painting them easier and less messy.

4. If the paint has settled in the bottle, gently roll the bottle on the table until mixed. Remove the lid and snip the tip of the bottle about $1/4$" down from the top. Start the flow of paint on a paper towel. Keep the tip of the bottle clean. Squeeze out the desired color of stained glass paint in the center of the wood shape. Work the paint to the edges with the tip of the bottle squeezing out more paint as needed to fill in the space. The paint should not go over the edge, but if it does just wipe off with cotton swab. Bubbles can be popped with the straight pin. Continue adding paint to all the pieces. Let dry.

5. Carefully peel the shapes from the tape and position in place on the frame. Glue in place on the frame. Hang and enjoy.

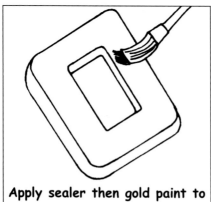

Apply sealer then gold paint to the front of the frame.

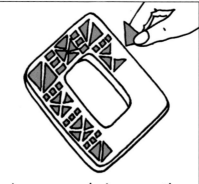

Arrange wood pieces on the frame in desired pattern.

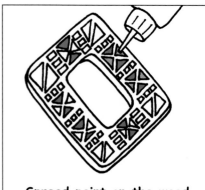

Spread paint on the wood pieces with tip.

Delta Paint Jewels™, Ceramcoat® Acrylic Paint, Gleams™, All Purpose Sealer; Forster® Woodsies™; Beacon™ Kids Choice Glue™; Fiskars® Scissors

Aqueducts

by Patty Cox

The land which surrounded Rome was abundant with springs. This water was channeled into the city of Rome through the channels of aqueducts. Large cisterns held the water at the end of the aqueducts and were used for baths and fountains.

You will need:
2 Sheets adhesive backed craft foam - 1 dark blue, 1 light blue
Pint jar
Scissors
2 Cups Epsom salt
1 Cup sea salt or rock salt
Food coloring
1/4 Teaspoon glycerine
Fragrance oil
Optional: Ribbon

1. Cut the smaller layer of arches from light blue foam according to pattern. Remove paper backing, then adhere to dark blue foam.

2. Cut blue foam about 1/8" larger all around to border the lighter foam shape, including the archway openings.

3. Cut rocks from the dark blue base color and stick around aqueduct arches.

4. Remove paper backing from blue foam arches, then adhere to the pint jar.

5. Fill jar with bath salts.

Optional: Tie ribbon around jar lid.

Bath Salt Recipe:

Mix epsom salt, sea salt or rock salt, a few drops of food coloring, glycerine and fragrance oil in a large bowl. Spoon or pour salts into pint jar. Screw lid on tightly.

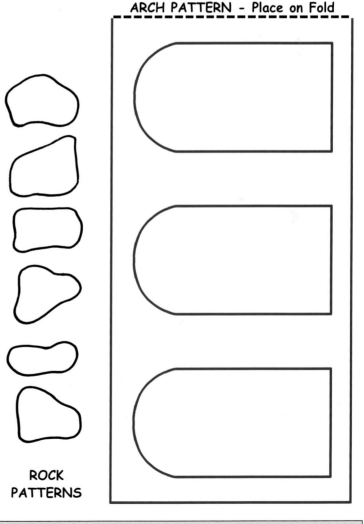

ARCH PATTERN - Place on Fold

ROCK PATTERNS

Darice® Adhesive Backed Foamies™; Fiskars® Scissors

Vellum Journal
by Sandi Genovese

Books were made of papyrus scrolls. Later parchment or vellum, a sheer paper was used to record events, write letters and make books.

You will need:
Die cut machine and dies
  or pattern and scissors
Dies - Star #1A, Circles
Paper - tan, ivory, white, green,
  gold, orange, red
Raffia
Black pen
Adhesive
$1/8$" Hole Punch

1. Using die cut machine or scissors, cut shapes from colored paper as shown on the patterns. Trim tan colored paper to 12" x 8" size, then fold in half across the width to measure 6" x 8".

2. Trim several sheets of white paper and a piece of vellum for first sheet so that they are smaller than the cover. Fold all sheets in half.

3. Punch two holes in the cover on the fold line about 1" from the edge. Using the cover holes as a guide, punch two holes along the fold line in the inside sheets.

4. With the vellum as the first sheet, align the sheets inside the cover, then thread raffia through the holes. Tie a bow on the outside.

5. Draw the pattern for the Roman border on heavy paper, then cut out.

6. Cut a piece of white paper about 2" smaller on all sides than the front cover. Trace the border around the edge of the paper. Color the negative black and leave the pattern white.

7. Center, then glue the bordered paper to a sheet of red paper that is slightly larger to make a red border around the edge. Cut out, then add a green square to each corner.

8. Place a red rectangle in the center. Attach a smaller white rectangle on top of the red.

9. To make a Roman shield, overlap then glue the two gold stars together. Glue red, white and gold circles in the middle. Glue the shield to the center of the white paper.

10. Mat the Roman design on ivory paper, then glue to the center of the journal cover.

Check out these web sites for additional Roman designs: www.grahamthomas.com/lyson3.html, www.3vwargames.co.uk/graphics/112.jpg

Ellison® XL Ellison® Letter Machine™, Instructional and Decorative Dies;
Strathmore Construction Paper

Trim sheets of paper. Fold in half. Punch holes on fold.

Assemble, then tie papers and cover together with raffia.

Glue Roman shield pattern to ivory paper.

Glue decorated panel to the cover of the book.

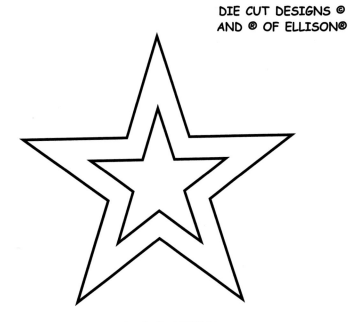

STAR PATTERN
CUT 2 - GOLD

SQUARE PATTERN
CUT 2 - GREEN

BORDER PATTERN

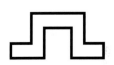

CIRCLE PATTERN
CUT 1 - GOLD

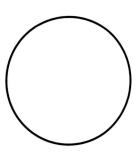

CIRCLE PATTERN
CUT 1 - WHITE

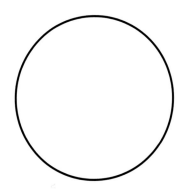

CIRCLE PATTERN
CUT 1 - RED

Samian Ware Tile

by Lorine Mason

Many homes were decorated with pottery wall decorations called reliefs. Different clays were used depending on the area. One style was called Samian Ware, a red clay pottery popular after A.D. 100.

You will need:
Terra cotta clay
6" Ceramic tile
White acrylic paint
Pencil with eraser
Plastic caps
Bamboo skewer
10" Leather lacing
9" x 12" Brown felt
Rolling pin
Soft rag
Glue
Scissors
Plastic knife

1. Knead clay until soft and smooth. Roll clay into a square slightly larger than the 6" tile. Lay the clay over the tile and wrap it around the edges.

2. Using the rolling pin, smooth the clay over the front and sides of the tile. Cut away any extra clay at the back of the tile with a plastic knife.

3. Trace, then cut out the urn pattern. Place pattern on top of the clay covered tile. Using a pencil, trace over the design lines on the pattern. Remove the pattern and using the skewer trace the design into the clay.

4. Create additional designs and borders by pressing into the clay with the skewer, plastic caps and eraser end of pencil.

5. Place the clay covered tile on an oven proof glass surface and bake in a 275°F oven for 15 minutes, with good ventilation. DO NOT USE MICROWAVE OVEN. Avoid over baking. Thicker pieces of clay may require additional baking time. Let cool.

6. Using a soft cloth, rub a small amount of white paint into the indentations on the front of the tile. Wipe off excess paint. Let dry.

7. Lay the tile on top of the felt. Trace around edges, then cut out.

9. Spread glue along the edges of the felt and lay the lacing in the glue at the top corners. Add a drop of glue to each end of lacing. Place the tile on top of the felt. Press slightly and let dry.

*Make sure to wash your hands and all surfaces after using clay.

Polyform Original Sculpey® Polymer Clay; Delta Ceramcoat® Acrylic Paint; Darice® Leather Lacing, and Felt; Fiskars® Scissors; Beacon™ Kids Choice Glue™

URN PATTERN

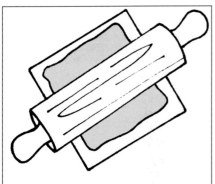

Smooth the clay on the tile
with the rolling pin.

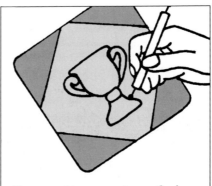

Place pattern on top of clay.
Trace around design.

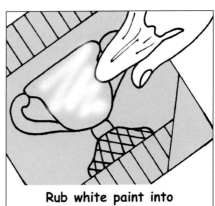

Rub white paint into
the pattern on the tile.

Marine Mosaic Tile

by Kathi Taylor Shearer

Because of the proximity to water, marine or sea themes were an important design element in Ancient Rome.

You will need:
4 1/4" Square white ceramic tile
Satin découpage medium
Die cut machine and die
  or pattern and scissors
White craft paper
Black construction paper
Blue shadow paper
Light blue marble paper
Scissors
Decorative edge scissors
1/8" Hole punch
Paintbrush
Pencil
Ruler

1. Seal top and sides of tile with one coat of découpage medium. Let dry.

2. Cut out dolphin, then trace pattern onto ceramic tile.

3. Punch a circle from black paper for the dolphin's eye. Using decorative edge scissors cut a strip of black paper approximately 1/8" wide. Trim the strip to fit the length of the dolphin's body. Apply découpage medium to the back and adhere to outlined shape of the dolphin's body as shown.

4. Cut paper mosaic "tiles" for dolphin's body from blue shadow paper. Cut tiles for background from light blue. The tiles are best cut in triangle shapes of varying sizes. Start by cutting 1/8" to 3/8" strips of paper. Cut strips of paper at different angles to create a variety of sizes and shapes of triangles.

5. Apply découpage medium to a small area of outlined dolphin shape on tile and cover area with triangle tiles, leaving small spaces between. Repeat process until dolphin body is complete.

6. Repeat step 5 to fill the background around the dolphin using light blue marble paper.

7. To seal, apply 3 to 4 coats of Decoupage medium to tile sides and surface. Allow to dry between coats.

8. Repeat steps 1 through 7 to make an Octopus tile if desired.

Delta Ceramcoat® Stain Decoupage Medium; Ellison® XL Ellison® Letter Machine™, Instructional and Decorative Dies; Strathmore Kids™ Series Construction Paper, Craft Paper, Shadow Paper, Pure Paper Marble Paper; Fiskars® Scissors, Paper Edgers, Hole Punch, Ruler

OCTOPUS PATTERN

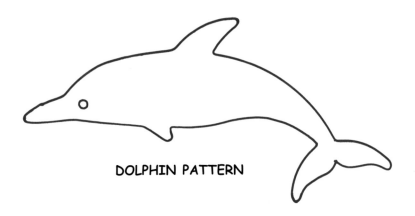

DOLPHIN PATTERN

DIE CUT DESIGNS ©
AND ® OF ELLISON®

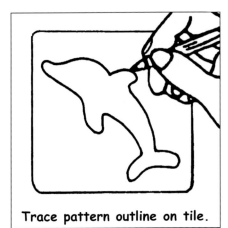

Trace pattern outline on tile.

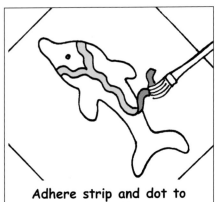

Adhere strip and dot to
dolphin image.

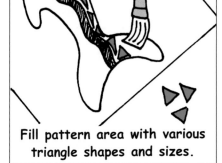

Fill pattern area with various
triangle shapes and sizes.

Roman Numeral Wrap Up

by Leslie Frederick

Various column styles which originated in Greece were also popular in Rome. The more decorated style was Corinthian which had the shape of leaves carved in the top.

You will need:
8 1/2" x 11" White cardboard
Embroidery floss
Permanent marker
Decorative corner scissors
Glue
Paper cutter
1/16" Hole punch

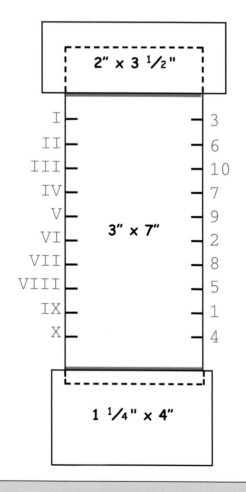

1. Cut one each of the following rectangles from white paper:

   3" x 7", 1 1/4" x 4", and 2" x 3 1/2".

2. Trim bottom corners of the two smaller rectangles with corner edgers.

3. Make a pencil mark 1" down from the top of large rectangle and 3/4" up from the bottom.

4. Glue 1 1/4" x 4" piece horizontally along top of column, placing bottom, decorated edge on 1" mark. Glue 2" x 3 1/2" piece horizontally along bottom of column placing decorated edge at 3/4" mark. Make a mark every 1/2" on both sides of column to mark the numbers as shown. Decorate if desired.

5. Using green marker, write Roman numerals as shown along left side. Write numbers as shown along right side. Decorate column with green marker.

6. Punch a hole in top right hand corner of column. Insert embroidery floss through hole and tie knot on front of the column.

7. Cut a 1/4" slit into the side of the column beside each number.

8. Starting with number "one", wind the floss around the column matching to the correct Roman numeral. Continue wrapping until all numbers are matched with Roman numerals.

9. Make sure all the Roman numerals and numbers are correctly matched. Turn the column over and trace the path of the floss back and forth with a pencil, then you'll know if you are correct in the future.

Fiskars® Corner Edgers, Personal Paper Trimmer, Scissors, Ruler & Hole Punch

Mayan Pot

by Lorine Mason

Mayans developed many traditional designs for pots and containers made from clay found in the Yucatan peninsula.

You will need:
Wire mesh
Plaster tape roll
Sand - black, white
Acrylic paint - beige, black
Plastic margarine container - 1/2 lb
Scissors
Paintbrush
Newspaper

1. Cut a piece of wire mesh large enough to go around your container. Stretch the mesh and mold around the plastic container. Slide the container out and carefully fold over the top edges of the mesh to the inside of the bowl shape. Shape the pot by squeezing in about an 1" from the top.

2. Cut a 2 foot section of plaster tape into 1" wide strips.

3. Cover your work surface with newspaper and fill the plastic container with warm water.

4. Dip one strip in the water at a time, then wrap around the mesh shape. Starting at the top edge, slightly overlap the strips as you lay them around the bowl. Smooth the surface as you work. Let dry.

5. Paint the entire bowl with beige paint.

6. Sprinkle white sand onto the wet paint. Let dry. Paint designs with black paint, then sprinkle black sand onto the wet paint. Let dry.

Stretch mesh around the plastic container.

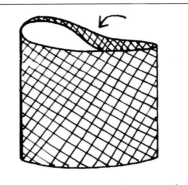

Fold over the top edges to the inside of the shape.

Lay strips over the mesh, overlapping slightly.

Activa® Activ-Wire Mesh, Rigid Wrap®, Scenic Sand®; Delta Ceramcoat® Acrylic Paint; Fiskars® Scissors

Headdress
by Dimples Mucherino

Mayans wore colorful headdresses for ceremonies. They prized the long blue green tail feathers of the Quetzel Whoe bird.

You will need:
12" x 16" Silver plastic backed foil sheets
White plastic visor
Two 54" lengths of both green and blue
  straw satin raffia
Feathers - 6 blue, 6 green
Assorted antique silver beads -
  2 each, 4 different styles

Rhinestones - 1 large, 2 medium
24 Pony beads - 6 each, 4 colors
Double stick tape
Glue
Scissors
Pencil
Ruler

1. Place foil face down on flat surface. Place visor face down on foil, centered from side to side and 1" from bottom edge. Trace around inside edge with pencil. Cut foil 1" wider than pencil line. Clip inside curves to pencil line. Fold foil around and cover back of visor. Trim excess if necessary. Tape edges in place.

2. Position, then glue rhinestones onto the front of the visor.

3. Holding ends together, take a piece of green and blue raffia and wind around end of visor. Tie in a knot, leaving approximately 10" hanging. Repeat on opposite side.

4. String one of each color pony bead and two different antique silver beads on each set of raffia ends. Tie a single knot below the beads. Insert feather quills into bead holes and under top outer edge of raffia on side of visor.

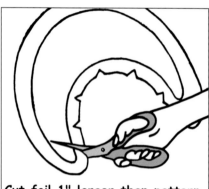

Cut foil 1" larger than pattern. Clip inside curves.

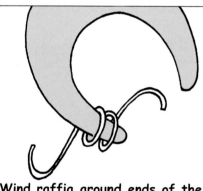

Wind raffia around ends of the visor. Knot to secure.

Insert feather quills into beads at ends of raffia.

Reynolds® Bright Ideas™ Ultra™ Foil Sheets, Double Sided Tape; Darice® Plastic Visor, Raffia, Feathers, Antique Beads, Rhinestones, Pony Beads; Fiskars® Scissors, Ruler

Stepped Frame
by Paula Bales

The Mayans built stepped pyramids with stairways leading to temples at the top. Usually they were built of limestone and were often painted red.

You will need:
Three 24" Basswood
  strips - $^3/_8$" x $^3/_8$"
24" Basswood sheet - $^3/_{16}$" x 1"
Wood cutting tool
Light brown sand
White glue
Ruler
Sanding block
$^1/_2$" Paintbrush
Wax paper

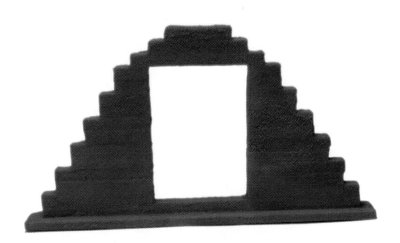

1. Referring to pattern, use the wood cutting tool to cut the following lengths of basswood strips:

one - 10", two - 3 $^1/_2$", five - 3", four - 2 $^1/_2$", five - 2", four - 1 $^1/_2$"", four - 1", and one - 4".

2. Cut one 11" piece from the basswood sheet for the base. Sand as needed.

3. Using the pattern as a guide, begin gluing the basswood strips on top of the basswood sheet to construct the frame.

4. Thin glue with the same amount of water. Paint the entire frame with the glue mixture. Before the glue dries, lay frame on wax paper and sprinkle sand heavily over glue.

5. Tape a picture to the back of the frame.

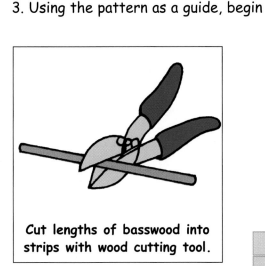

Cut lengths of basswood into strips with wood cutting tool.

2"	
3"	
4"	
1"	1"
1"	1"
1 $^1/_2$"	1 $^1/_2$"
1 $^1/_2$"	1 $^1/_2$"
2"	2"
2"	2"
2 $^1/_2$"	2 $^1/_2$"
2 $^1/_2$"	2 $^1/_2$"
3"	3"
3"	3"
3 $^1/_2$"	3 $^1/_2$"
10"	
11"	

Midwest Products Co., Inc. Micro-Cut® Quality Woods, Sanding Block, Easy Cutter and Super Easy Cutter; Activa® Scenic Sand®; Fiskars® Ruler' Beacon™ Kids Choice Glue™

Astronomy Wall Hanging
by Leslie Frederick

The Maya developed a calendar system based on the movement of the moon and stars. They are known for their astronomy skills.

You will need:
2mm Foam sheets - blue, yellow
Die cut machine and dies
   or pattern and scissors
Craft wire - yellow, blue
12-18 Beads - glow in the dark colors
$1/4$" Dowel
$1/16$" Hole punch
Silver acrylic paint
Paintbrush
Craft snips

1. Using die cut machine and dies, or pattern and scissors, cut one moon from blue foam. Cut one rabbit, one large star, four small stars and one large sun shape from yellow foam.

2. Using craft snips, cut a 12" length of dowel. Apply two coats of silver paint to dowel. Let dry between coats.

3. Punch a hole at the top of each foam shape.

4. Cut the wire into several different lengths, between 8" and 12".

5. Insert wire into hole in die cuts. Add beads then twist wire around pencil to create coils and twists. Wrap wire ends around dowel, spacing evenly along length of dowel.

6. Pull shapes gently to different lengths as shown in photo.

7. To create a loop for hanging your design, cut an extra long length of wire, approximately 24" long and coil around both ends of dowel. Embellish the loop with additional stars. Add extra stars to pieces of wire and wrap those around loop as shown. Allow glow in the dark beads to absorb some light, then turn out the lights and enjoy your creation.

Thread wire through shapes, add beads then coil.

Pull shapes so that wires are different lengths.

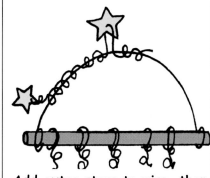

Add extra stars to wire, then wrap around loop.

Darice® Foamies™, Glow In The Dark Beads; Ellison® The Ellison® XL Letter Machine™, Decorative and Instructional Dies;Toner Plastics Inc.™ Fun Wire™; Delta Ceramcoat®Acrylic Paint;Forster® Dowel; Fiskars® Scissors, Hole Punch and Craft Snips

SMALL STAR PATTERN
CUT 4 YELLOW

LARGE SUN PATTERN
CUT 1 YELLOW

LARGE STAR PATTERN
CUT 1 YELLOW

MOON PATTERN
CUT 1 BLUE

RABBIT PATTERN
CUT 1 YELLOW

DIE CUT DESIGNS ©
AND ® OF ELLISON®

Stela
by Patty Cox

A Mayan Stela is a monument carved in stone commemorating significant people and events in history.

You will need:
White or terra cotta clay
28" Length black craft lace
Mini craft stick
Plastic fork
Chalk

STELA PATTERN

LARK'S HEAD KNOT

1. Knead clay until soft and smooth. Roll clay into $1/8$" wide snakes. Cut snakes into the following lengths, then coil each according to patterns.

   Two eyes - 4" each; two eyebrows - 5" each;

   One mouth - 7"; two ears - 3" each;

   Two feet - 5" each

2. Roll clay into two $1/4$" balls for crown top and forehead dot. Roll clay into nine $3/8$" balls for earrings, crown top center and nose. Shape nose into triangle.

3. Score sides of each piece with fork. Press clay pieces together according to pattern. Press sides of feet into squares using a craft stick.

4. Make a small hole at the top of the stela at center with a pencil.

5. Bake on an oven proof glass surface at 275°F for 15 minutes per $1/4$" thickness, with good ventilation. DO NOT USE MICROWAVE OVEN. Avoid over baking. Thicker pieces may require additional baking time. Let cool.

6. To antique stela, rub chalk over raised areas of clay. Rub chalk into clay with fingers.

7. Fold lacing in half, then insert end through stela hole. Tie a lark's head knot in lacing for the necklace.

Polyform Original Sculpey® Polymer Clay; Toner Plastics, Inc.™ CraftLace™;
Craf-T Products Chalk

Mayan Shirt

by Barb Zimmerman

Mayans were known for their weaving skills. This traditional shirt incorporates texture and color for a traditional Mayan design.

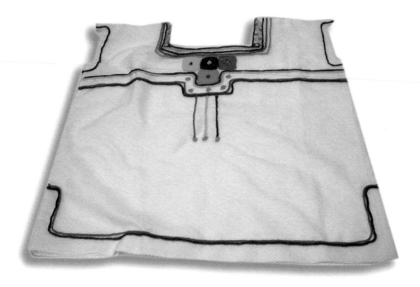

You will need:

White pillow case
Yarn - red, orange, purple, and green
Fabric glue

Pinking shears
Scissors
Tape measure
Wax paper

1. Prewash pillow case to remove sizing. Dry.

2. Using pinking shears, cut a neck opening and two armholes. Cut approximately 10" off the bottom of the pillow case using pinking shears.

3. Cut lengths of different colored yarn to form your desired pattern around the neck opening and across the front of the shirt. Apply a bead of fabric glue and adhere the yarn to the pillow case. The glue dries quickly so only apply glue a section at a time. Let dry.

Hint: Slide a piece of wax paper inside pillow case while gluing. Remove once the glue dries.

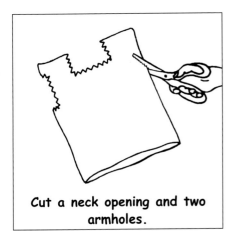

Cut a neck opening and two armholes.

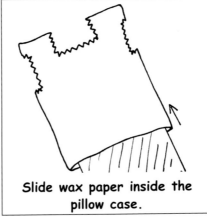

Slide wax paper inside the pillow case.

Attach yarn design with a bead of glue.

Fiskars® Pinking Shears, Scissors; Beacon™ Fabri-Tac™

Coins

by Beth Wheeler

Coins were a means of trading and were made from various metals. Often Runic symbols were embossed into the surface.

You will need:

Empty cereal box, or cardboard
Quart size empty milk carton - clean and dry
Plastic backed foil - 1 sheet each, blue and silver
Four 1 ½" wooden knobs
Gold acrylic paint
Stylus
Scissors
Double stick tape
Paintbrush
Glue

1. Open the serving end of the milk carton. Cut out the flap with the screw cap, if there is one, then cut a 2" x ½" slit in one side of carton.

2. Fold the remaining flaps flat, then secure with tape.

3. Cover carton with blue, plastic backed foil, wrapping like a gift. Secure to the carton with double stick tape. Carefully cut a slit in the foil over the slit in the carton, then fold to inside of bank through the slit with your fingers.

4. Apply paint to rounded edges of knobs, leaving flat side unpainted. Let dry.

5. Glue flat side of knobs to bottom of carton at each corner.

6. Using pattern, cut about six, 1 ½" circles from the cereal box.

7. Place cardboard circles on the wrong side of silver foil, then trace around the edge with a stylus. Cut out each circle adding about ½" to wrap around.

8. Place coin pattern on the coin circles, then trace over the lines with a stylus.

9. Wrap one embossed foil circle around each cardboard circle. Secure cut edges to wrong side with double stick tape. Glue coins on top of the bank.

10. Add desired embossing details to top of coin bank with stylus.

Reynolds® Bright Ideas™ Ultra™ Foil Sheets, Stylus, Double Sided Tape; Delta Ceramcoat® Acrylic Paint; Fiskars® Scissors; Darice® Wood Knobs

Cut flap with screw cap from end of milk carton.

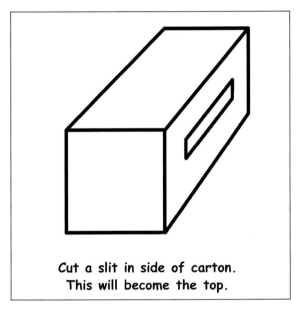

Cut a slit in side of carton. This will become the top.

Wrap carton with foil.

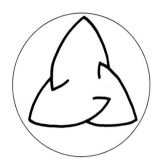

COIN PATTERN
FRONT

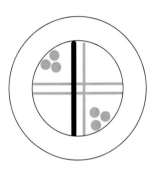

COIN PATTERN
BACK

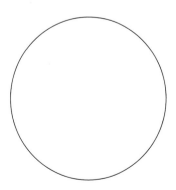

CIRCLE PATTERN
FOR COIN

Weather Vane
by Dimples Mucherino

Carved weather vanes were mounted on the front of Longboats as a navigational aid.

You will need:
1/4" x 12" Wood dowel
Wood ghost shapes - 14 small,
 2 medium, 4 large
Large Wood candy corn shape
Small Wood candy corn shape
2 1/2" x 1/2" Wood craft disk
2" Wood ball knob
5/8" Wood mini candle cup
9" Length 18 gauge craft wire
Acrylic paint - black, blue, white
Craft drill with 1/16" drill bit
Black permanent marker
Flat paintbrush
Ruler
Glue

1. Glue flat edge of ball knob to center of craft disk. Glue mini candle cup to center top of ball knob. Set aside.

2. Glue two small ghosts together, back to back. Repeat to make 7 glued pairs. These will be the tail. Glue medium and large ghosts together as pictured for the body. Glue one tail section to back side of body. Glue second tail section to back of previous one. Glue remaining tail sections together in same manner. Glue small candy corn to back of last tail section. Glue large candy corn head in place on front of body.

3. Cut 1/4" dowel in half. Ask an adult to drill a hole through dowel 1" from cut end.

4. Thread wire through drilled hole. Bend the wire to form N on one end and a point on the opposite end.

5. Glue top of dowel to the center of the Seahorse at the back. Glue opposite end into the candle cup.

6. Paint base and dowel black. Paint front and back of Seahorse blue. Use end of a paintbrush to apply dots of white paint to body. Add details to the body and face with a black marker.

Forster® Wood Dowels, Woodsies™; Darice® Craftwood™; Toner Plastics, Inc.™ Fun Wire™; Delta Ceramcoat® Acrylic Paint; Beacon™ Kids Choice Glue™; Fiskars® Craft Drill, Ruler

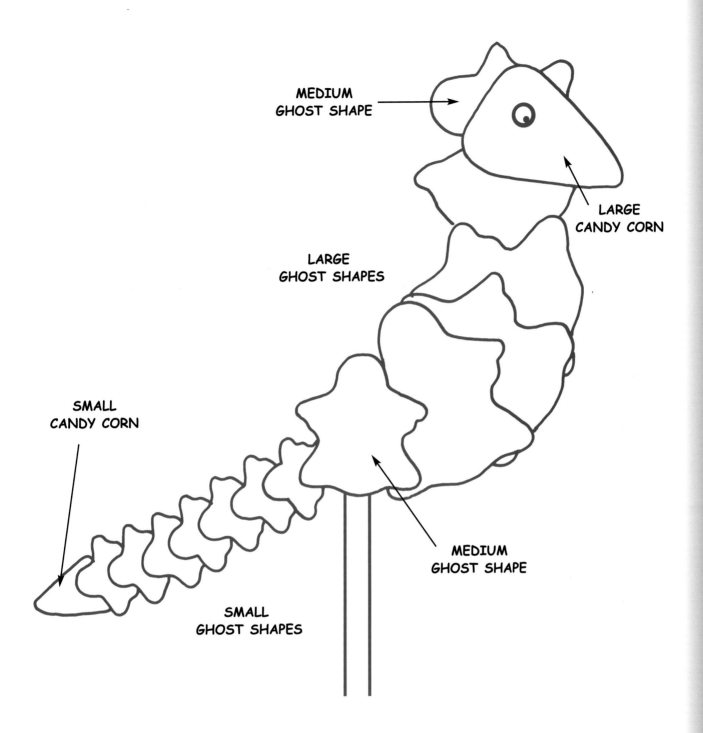

MEDIUM
GHOST SHAPE

LARGE
CANDY CORN

LARGE
GHOST SHAPES

SMALL
CANDY CORN

MEDIUM
GHOST SHAPE

SMALL
GHOST SHAPES

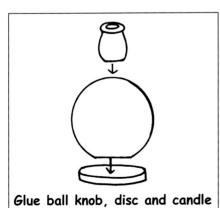

Glue ball knob, disc and candle cup together.

Glue ghost shapes together to form tail.

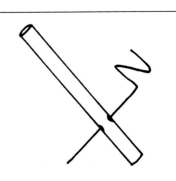

Thread wire through hole. Form "N" at one end.

Helmet

by Lorine Mason

Defensive equipment such as helmets were very important since Vikings often fought hand to hand. Helmet designs varied from a simple iron mask with a riveted nose guard to more elaborate styles.

You will need:
Instant papier maché
Wire mesh
Plaster tape roll
Acrylic paint - gray, black
Balloon
Scissors
Black permanent marker
Rolling pin
Paintbrush
Craft stick
Soft rag
Large plastic freezer bag
String
Plastic wrap

1. Blow up a balloon and tie a 12" piece of string to the end.

2. Measure 4 cups of instant paper maché into the freezer bag. Add 1 ½ cups of water. Close the bag and mix paper maché inside the bag to form clay.

3. Cover your work surface with plastic wrap. Empty the contents of the freezer bag on top of the plastic wrap and continue to mix the clay. When the clay is mixed, flatten it, then cover with another piece of plastic wrap. Use a rolling pin to roll out the paper maché in a 16" circle.

4. Pick up the rolled out clay and lay it over the balloon. Smooth the clay over the balloon, carefully cutting away excess clay. Dip your hands into water and smooth any seams or bumps. Use a craft stick to help smooth the surface. Hang the balloon upside down to dry overnight.

5. Shape the horn pieces by cutting two 4"x4" strips of wire mesh. Form a roll and then pinch one end. Curve the mesh to resemble a horn. Repeat for a second horn.

6. Pop the balloon. Draw a line around the paper maché shape to create the bowl shape helmet. Cut on the line.

7. Cover your work surface with newspaper. Cut twenty-five 1" strips of plaster cloth. Fill a bowl with warm water. Dip one strip in the water at a time and wrap around the horn shape. Start at the bottom edge and lay strips overlapping each other. Smooth the surface as you work. Let dry.

8. Cut forty 1" strips of plaster cloth. Dip one strip in the water at a time and attach the horns to the helmet. Continue adding strips to helmet. Add a raised center ridge and bottom edge to the helmet by adding extra strips along the bottom edge and down the center. Let dry.

9. Paint the entire helmet gray. Let dry.

10. To make the helmet look old, apply a thin coat of black paint. Wipe with a soft cloth, allowing paint to remain only in the crevices.

Activa® Activ-Wire Mesh, Rigid Wrap®, Celluclay®; Delta Ceramcoat® Acrylic Paint; Fiskars® Scissors

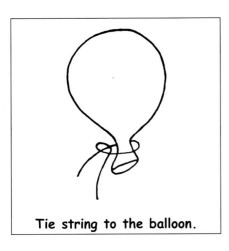

Tie string to the balloon.

Mix papier maché and water in a freezer bag.

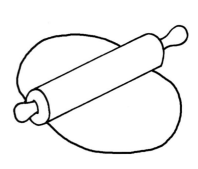

Roll clay into a circle with a rolling pin.

Lay the clay over the top of the balloon.

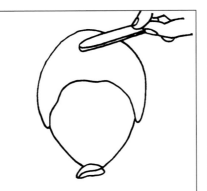

Smooth the clay with a craft stick.

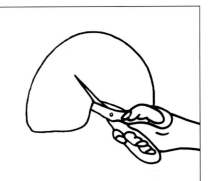

Cut out helmet shape from dried paper maché clay.

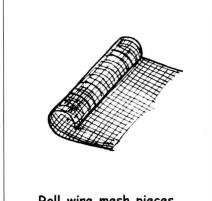

Roll wire mesh pieces.

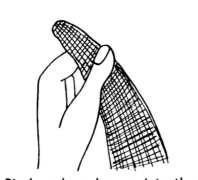

Pinch ends and curve into the shape of a horn.

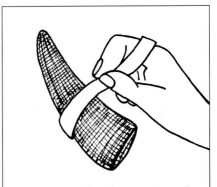

Cover mesh with strips of plaster cloth.

Attach horns to helmet with strips of plaster cloth.

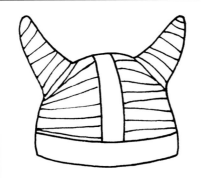

Place extra strips down center and along the edge for ridges.

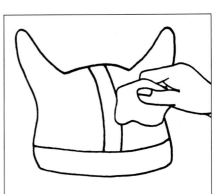

Paint with black paint then wipe off with a soft cloth.

Runic Bracelet

by Patty Cox

Runic writings were carved in stone, bone, horn wood, and on metal and coins. These inscriptions often contained information about a person, such as their voyages, family, wealth, and talents. The word "rune" comes from a Gothic word meaning secrets.

You will need:	
Plastic backed holographic sheets -2 different colors	Embroidery floss
	Hole punch
	Double stick tape
Black permanent marker	Scissors

1. Cut a $5/8$" x $5 1/4$" strip of holographic foil for bracelet top layer. Tape strip to a second color. Cut strip $1/8$" larger all around.

2. Punch holes in each end of bracelet. Cut two 6" lengths of embroidery floss. Secure threads in each hole with a lark's head knot.

3. Refer to the Runic alphabet below. Using black marker, write name or message on bracelet. Some letters from our alphabet are not included in the runic alphabet. Use a letter/symbol that sounds like the missing letter. Example: C=S or K, Q = K, Y = E.

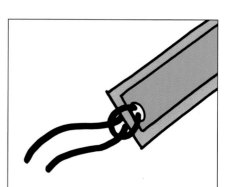

Attach embroidery floss to each end of bracelet.

RUNIC ALPHABET

ᚠ ᚢ ᚦ ᚨ ᚱ ᚲ ᚷ ᚹ ᚺ ᚾ ᛁ ᛃ ᛈ ᛇ ᛊ ᛏ ᛒ ᛖ ᛗ ᛚ ᛜ ᛞ ᛟ

f u b a r k g w h n l j p e r s t b e m i ng d o

Reynolds® Bright Ideas™ Holographic Sheets, Double Sided Tape; Fiskars® Hole Punch, Scissors

Pagoda Frame
by Mary Ayres

The Shitennoji Pagoda is the oldest Buddhist temple in Japan. It was built in 593 AD. Temple guard statues stand in a fighting position at the opening of the pagoda.

You will need:
3 Colored wood craft sticks
2 Colored mini wood craft sticks
Flat wood shapes - large square,
  medium square, large triangle,
  2 medium and 2 small triangles
Acrylic paint - lilac, black
5 Gold 8mm sequins
Gold metallic ridged craft paper
Decorative edge scissors
Glue
Masking tape
Paintbrush

1. Paint squares lilac. Paint triangles black. Let dry. **Hint**: To paint shapes easily, wrap masking tape around fingers, sticky side out. Stick wood shape to tape and paint.

2. Place 2 craft sticks on work surface for sides of pagoda. Glue a mini craft stick across bottom of side sticks. Glue remaining craft stick across top of side sticks with ends even on both sides, to form frame edge.

3. To assemble top of pagoda, glue remaining mini craft stick across the top of the large square with ends even on both sides. Glue the medium square centered on top of the mini craft stick. Let dry. Glue large square centered on top of frame shape. Glue a medium triangle to each end of the craft stick under large square. Glue a small triangle to each end of the mini craft stick under the medium square. Glue large triangle to the top of the medium square. Let dry.

4. Using decorative edge scissors, cut a ¼" wide strip from ridged paper (ridges should run up and down on strip). Cut strip into a length that is slightly longer than the large triangle, and glue to bottom of large triangle. Cut another ¼" wide strip into a length that is slightly

larger than a mini craft stick and glue on top of the mini craft stick that is under the medium square. Cut a ½" wide strip from ridged paper. Cut strip into a length that is slightly longer than a craft stick, and glue on top of the craft stick that is under the large square.

5. Glue a sequin to the top of the large triangle, and to the tip of each of the small and medium triangles. Let dry.

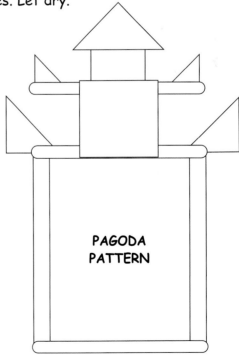

PAGODA
PATTERN

Delta Ceramcoat® Acrylic Paint; Darice® Colored Craft Sticks, Sequins; Forster® Woodsies™; Strathmore Kids™ Series Groovy Paper; Fiskars® Paper Edgers; Beacon™ Kids Choice Glue™

Bunraku

by Lorine Mason

Bunraku is a type of Japanese puppet theatre. It developed from storytelling to a musical form in the 16th century. Bunraku stories are usually about Japanese myths and folk tales. Large puppets are operated by people dressed in black so they cannot be seen against a black background.

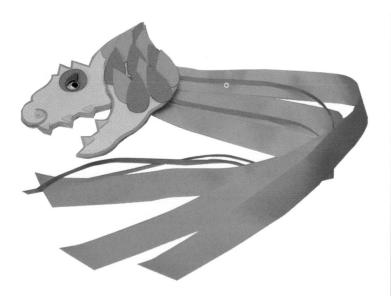

You will need:
6mm White foam sheet
3mm Foam sheets - orange, red
  and yellow
Foam craft shapes
15mm Wiggle eye
Orange permanent marker
1 ¹/₂" Metal brads
Glue
Fabric glue
Scissors
Ball point pen
¹/₈" Hole punch
Ribbon - 3 colors, 24" lengths each
Elastic

1. Trace, then cut out pattern from white foam. Punch holes at the marks.

2. Punch holes in the center of two circle foam shapes. Glue the circles over the punched hole on the upper jaw section of the puppet.

3. Decorate the puppet with foam shapes. Use the shapes as patterns to create additional pieces in other colors. Glue wiggle eyes in place.

4. Insert the metal brad through the holes at the jaw line.

5. Cut ribbons 24" in length and glue to the bottom edge at the back of the puppet.

6. Form two, 2" lengths of elastic into loops. Overlap ends, then secure with glue. Glue to the back of top and bottom sections of the puppet. Let dry.

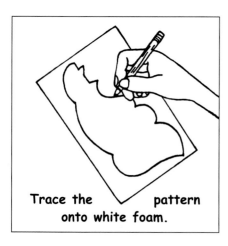

Trace the   pattern onto white foam.

Join pieces by inserting brad through holes at jaw line.

Form 2" loops from elastic. Overlap ends, then glue.

Darice® Foamies™, Wiggle Eyes, Metal Brads; Beacon™ Fabri-Tac™, Craft Foam Glue™; Fiskars® Hole Punch, Scissors

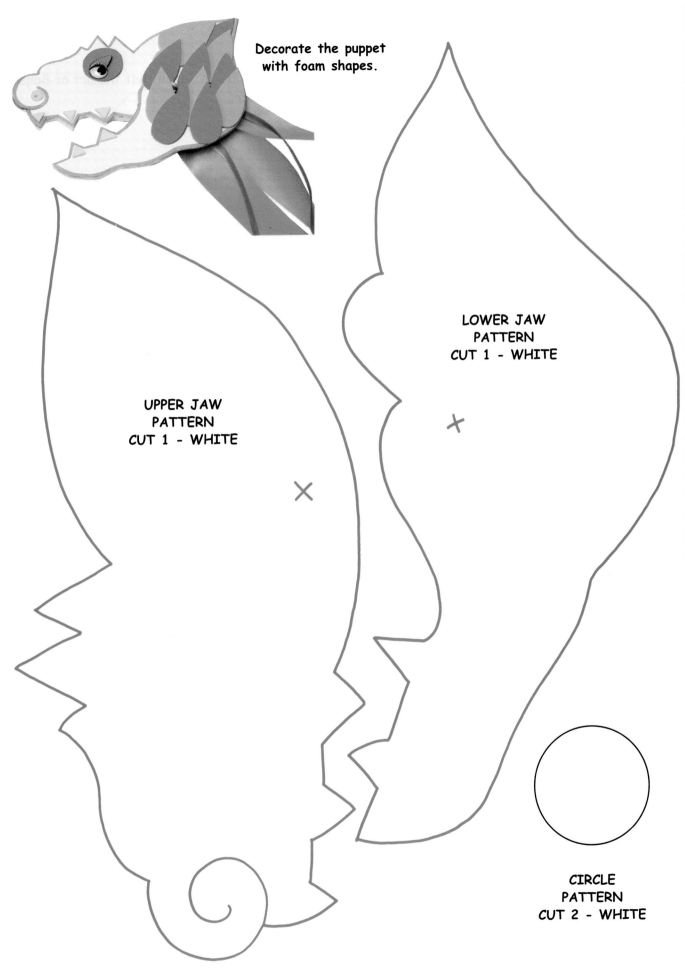

Decorate the puppet
with foam shapes.

UPPER JAW
PATTERN
CUT 1 - WHITE

LOWER JAW
PATTERN
CUT 1 - WHITE

CIRCLE
PATTERN
CUT 2 - WHITE

Paper Lanterns

by Cheryl Ball

Paper lanterns have been used in Japanese homes and festivals for centuries. Hand crafted of bamboo and paper, they come in all shapes and sizes.

You will need:
Acrylic paint - orange, red,
  white, yellow, pink
Rubber flower stamp
Stencil sponges
Vellum paper - assorted
  bright colors
Decorative edge scissors
1/4" Hole punch
Embossing tool
Silk ivy vine
String of twinkle lights
Double stick tape
Scissors
Pencil
Tracing paper
Ruler
Cotton swab

1. Trace and cut the patterns for the lanterns using tracing paper.

2. Trace the different shaped lanterns on different colors of vellum paper. Trace enough for the string of lights. Cut out.

3. Lay the ruler on the fold lines and trace over the line with the small end of the embossing tool. This will crease the paper and will make folding easier. Be careful not to press too hard so it doesn't tear the vellum. Continue with all the lanterns. Trim the bottom edge of each lantern with the decorative edge scissors.

4. Squeeze out acrylic paint on a plate. Tap the flat end of the stencil sponge into one of the paint colors, tapping excess off on the plate. Pounce the paint onto the design area of the rubber flower stamp. Press the flower stamp onto a lantern shape. Carefully lift and repeat the process on each lantern in a random design. Refer to the photo for placement and colors. Use the cotton swab to add a dot of contrasting paint color into the center of each flower. Let dry.

5. Punch a hole in the top of each lantern using the hole punch. Carefully fold the lantern together, securing the flaps with double stick tape.

6. Wind the string of lights around the ivy vine.

7. To attach the lanterns to the lights, have an adult remove the bulb from each socket. Push the socket through the hole in the top of the lantern, then replace the bulb. Hang and enjoy.

Delta Ceramcoat® Acrylic Paint, Rubber Stampede® Design Elements, Stencil Sponges; Strathmore Bright Translucent Vellum, Tracing Paper; Fiskars® Paper Edgers, Hole Punch, Scissors, Embossing Tool

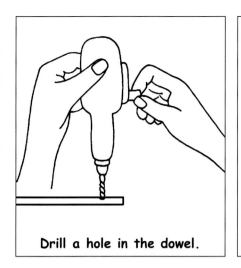

Drill a hole in the dowel.

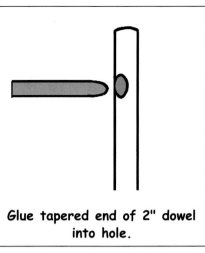

Glue tapered end of 2" dowel into hole.

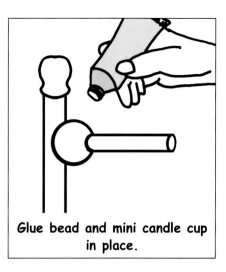

Glue bead and mini candle cup in place.

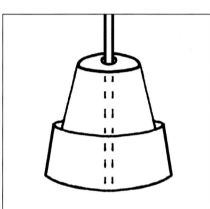

Push dowel into hole in flower pot until end is even with rim.

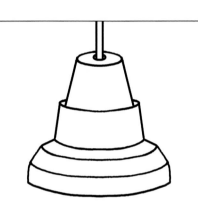

Glue flower pot upside down to center of upturned saucer.

Glue large diamonds to flat side of wood wheel.

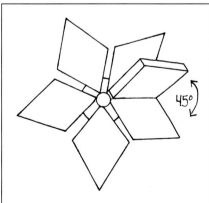

Glue medium diamonds between large diamonds at 45° angle.

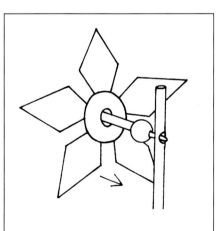

Slide wheel onto 2" dowel.

Glue bead onto end of dowel.

Darice® Craftwood™ Flower Pot, Candle Cup, Round Beads, Wheel; Forster® Wood Dowels, Woodsies™; Delta Ceramcoat® Gleams™ Acrylic Paint; Fiskars® Craft Drill, Softouch® Craft Snips, Ruler; Beacon™ Kids Choice Glue™

Battle Shield
by Beth Wheeler

Knights represented the feudal system. Metal was boiled in wax to form a shield with an embossed design.

You will need:
8" x 10" Corrugated cardboard
4" x 6" Non-corrugated cardboard
Plastic backed foil sheets -
  bronze and silver
Holographic stickers
Double stick tape
Thumbtacks or upholstery tacks
Permanent marker
Stylus
Scissors
Paper clip
Glue

1. Place large pattern on corrugated cardboard. Place smaller pattern on non-corrugated cardboard. Trace with pencil and cut out.

2. Place large cardboard piece on back of bronze foil sheet. Trace with stylus. Cut out $1/2$" bigger than traced line all around. Wrap foil around corrugated cardboard, securing to back with double stick tape.

3. Place smaller cardboard piece on back of bronze foil sheet. Trace with a stylus. Cut out $1/2$" larger than the traced line all around. Wrap foil around cardboard, securing to back with double stick tape. **Option:** Crumple the foil then flatten out for a hammered metal look.

4. Place large pattern on wrong side of silver foil. Trace with stylus. Cut out $1/2$" larger than traced line all around. Wrap foil around cardboard, securing to back with double stick tape.

5. Attach the small shield to the large shield with double stick tape.

6. Place thumbtacks around edge of shield.

7. Emboss shield as shown, or with similar designs. Add stickers as desired.

8. Write name at center with a marker.

9. Glue a paper clip on the top back of the shield for a hanger.

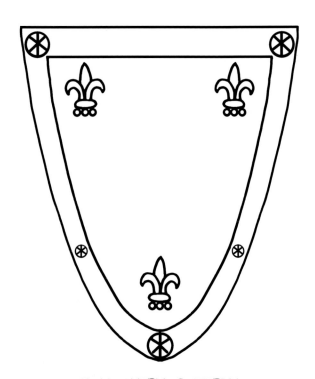

SMALL SHIELD PATTERN

Reynolds® Bright Ideas™ Ultra™ Foil Sheets, Stylus, Double Sided Tape, Holographic Stickers; Fiskars® Scissors

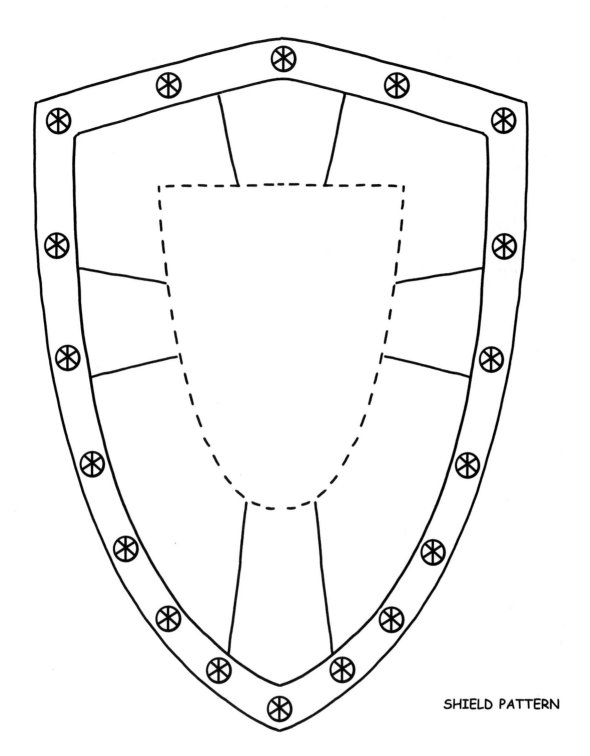

SHIELD PATTERN

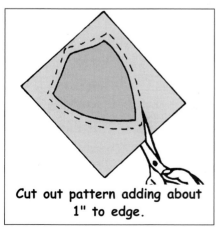

Cut out pattern adding about 1" to edge.

Attach foil to back with double stick tape.

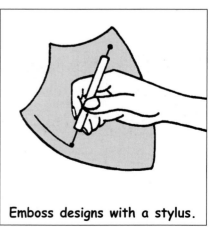

Emboss designs with a stylus.

Tournament Flag
by Paula Bales

Events were held between castles which included jousting. Flags with the crests of the families or castles were carried to identify the group in tournaments. Heraldry designs identified friends and enemies in battles.

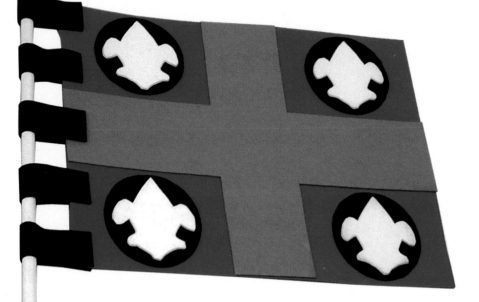

You will need:
2mm Blue foam
2mm Adhesive backed foam - black, white, light green
Die cut machine and die or patterns and scissors
White acrylic paint
³/₈" x 36" Dowel
Craft snips
Ruler
¹/₂" Paintbrush

1. Using die cut machine or pattern and scissors, cut 4 Fleur de Lis from white foam and one from light green foam. Using a ruler and pencil trace, then cut the cross pattern on light green foam. Cut four - 3" circles and five - 1" x 4 ¹/₂" strips from black foam.

2. Using craft snips, cut dowel 24" long. Paint dowel white. Let dry.

3. Referring to photo for placement, remove the backing from the adhesive backed foam shapes, then place the cross, circles and white Fleur de Lis on the blue foam sheet.

4. Peel off backing, then attach one end of each black foam strip to the left side of flag at the back, leaving approximately 1" between each strip. Wrap strips around dowel, then attach each one to the front of the flag.

5. Place light green Fleur de Lis at top of dowel.

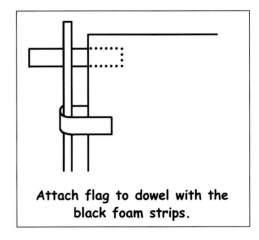

Attach flag to dowel with the black foam strips.

Darice® Foamies™; Ellison® XL Ellison™ Letter Machine™, Instructional and Decorative Dies; Delta Ceramcoat® Acrylic Paint; Midwest Products, Inc. Dowel; Fiskars® Scissors, Ruler

FLEUR DE LIS PATTERN
Cut 5
4 White
1 Light Green

CROSS PATTERN
Extend length and width to
fit blue foam sheet

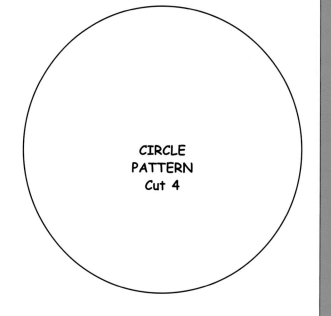

**CIRCLE
PATTERN
Cut 4**

DIE CUT DESIGNS ©
AND ® OF ELLISON®

Shop Sign

by Cheryl Ball

The Middle Ages was the time of the craftsman. Shop owners developed signs, many embossed in wood, to identify their craft. To be a citizen, you had to be in one of the 21 useful trades.

You will need:
Wood plaque or scrap wood piece
Acrylic paint - white, light green,
  green, pink, yellow, purple,
  orange and blue
All purpose sealer
Satin interior varnish
Alphabet stencils
Wood shapes:
  9 medium ovals, 2 large ovals,
  10 small circles, 2 medium circles,
  17 small tear drops, 5 medium
  tear drops, 10 large tear drops
Stencil sponges
2 craft sticks
Glue
Cardboard
Double stick tape
Scissors
White gel pen
Sanding block
Two screw eyes
1 Yard ribbon - any color
Flat paint brush
Blue masking tape

1. Apply a coat of sealer to the wood plaque. Let dry, then sand smooth. Paint the top of the wood with two coats of white. Allow paint to dry between coats. Paint the outside edge light green. Let dry. Varnish with a coat of satin varnish. Let dry.

2. Apply strips of double stick tape to the cardboard. Press the wood shapes onto it to make the painting easier and less messy. Paint the shapes in the following colors:

Pink - 9 medium ovals, 1 small circle

Blue - 8 large teardrops, 1 medium circle

Orange - 9 small teardrops

Purple - 8 small teardrops

Light green - 2 large ovals, 2 medium
  teardrops, 2 craft sticks

White - 9 small circles

Green - 3 medium teardrops, 2 large
  teardrops

Yellow - 1 medium circle

3. Varnish all wood pieces. Let dry.

4. Referring to picture, detail painted wood shapes with white gel pen. Carefully remove shapes from cardboard and position on plaque. Arrange the wood pieces on the plaque in the desired design, then glue in place.

5. To stencil on the name, first mask off the adjoining letters from the first letter being used with blue masking tape. Position the letter on the wood. Dip stencil sponge into purple paint, tapping off excess. Lightly pounce the sponge onto the stencil applying an even coat. Carefully remove the stencil. Let dry before moving to next letter. Continue stencilling all the letters, changing colors for each word.

6. Screw the screw eyes into the top of the board, then attach ribbons, trim ends and hang.

Delta Ceramcoat® Acrylic Paint, Satin Interior Varnish, All Purpose Sealer, Stencil Magic® Whimsical Dot Alphabet, Stencil Sponges; Forster® Woodsies™; Fiskars® Scissors

FLOWER PATTERN B
Shown smaller than actual size.

FLOWER PATTERN A
Shown smaller than actual size.

Mask off adjacent letters, then
stencil one letter at a time.

Faux Marble Heraldry Journal
by Sandy Laipply

Heraldry was an important part of the Middle Ages. Since many people could not write, their symbol became their signature.

You will need:
Journal or notebook
Watercolor paper
Acrylic paint - black, white and a
    third color of your choice
Faux finish glaze
Satin varnish
Die cut machine and die
    or pattern and scissors
Gold adhesive backed paper
Glue
1" Foam brush
Brown grocery bag
Newspaper
2 Cotton swabs
Ruler
Pencil

1. Measure, then cut watercolor paper large enough to cover front of journal.

2. Dribble both black and white paints in a diagonal line on watercolor paper. Immediately pounce with crunched up newspaper to mix. Do not over mix. Cover entire surface, adding additional paint as necessary.

3. Pull most of the cotton from a swab. Put a small puddle of both white and black paint on a paper plate. Dip the bare end of the swab into the white and drag through the marbled paint on your paper to create veins. Repeat with a second swab using the black paint. Veins should be loose and spidery. Let dry.

4. Lightly rub over the marbled surface with a piece of brown grocery bag. This will smooth out any large bumps of paint.

5. Mix equal amounts of desired paint color and clear glaze, then paint over marbled surface with a foam brush. Deepen the color if desired, with additional coats of glaze. Let dry between coats.

6. Using die cut machine or pattern and scissors, cut the lion shape from gold adhesive backed paper. Set the lion shape aside. Remove protective paper, then adhere the lion in center of the marbled paper. Carefully position eyes and mouth in lion's face. Apply a coat of varnish. Allow to dry.

7. Use a piece of cardboard to spread glue over entire surface of journal. Press marbled paper in place. Cover with wax paper and weigh down until dry.

Strathmore Kids™ Series Gel Jotter Paint Pad;
Ellison® XL Ellison® Letter Machine™, Instructional and Decorative Dies; Delta Ceramcoat® Acrylic Paints,
Faux Finish Glaze Base, Exterior/Interior Satin Varnish; Fiskars® Scissors, Ruler

Drizzle black and white paint over the watercolor paper.

Pounce with crumpled newspaper.

Remove cotton from swab then use to draw vein lines.

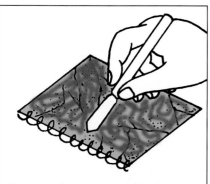

Coat surface of marbled paper with glaze mix.

LION PATTERN

3D Decoder Glasses

by Patty Cox

The first dual eyeglass lenses mounted in frames appeared about 1285 in Italy.

You will need:
Patchwork textured craft paper
Die cut machine and die
  or pattern and scissors
2" x 5" clear acetate

White paper
Wide tip red marker
Turquoise colored pencil
Red stamp pad and stamp
Glue

1. Using a die cut machine or pattern and scissors, cut glasses from textured paper. Glue ear pieces on sides of glasses.

2. Color one side of acetate with red wide tip marker. Trim acetate to fit into frames of glasses. Glue inside frames.

3. Write a message on white paper using a turquoise colored pencil.

4. Stamp over message with a rubber stamp and red ink stamp pad.

5. Wear the glasses and read the message.

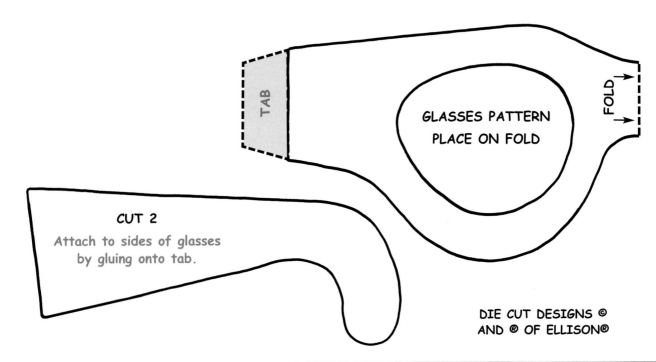

TAB

GLASSES PATTERN
PLACE ON FOLD

FOLD

CUT 2
Attach to sides of glasses
by gluing onto tab.

DIE CUT DESIGNS ©
AND ® OF ELLISON®

Ellison® XL Ellison® Letter Machine™, Instructional and Decorative Dies;
Strathmore Papers Kids™ Series Patch Paper; Fiskars® Scissors, Pigment Stamp Pad

Landscape
by Paula Bales

Landscapes were scenes of country life that became popular during the 15th century as wealthy families went to the countryside for vacation.

You will need:
Shadow construction paper - blue, green, black
Patch paper - green, light brown
Corduroy paper - dark green, light brown, maroon
Gray stone washed paper
Vellum - blue, white
Tracing paper
Scissors
Paper glue
Optional: decorative edge scissors

1. Transfer patterns onto tracing paper, then cut out.

2. Write the pattern numbers on the papers as follows: No. 1 on blue vellum, No. 2 on white vellum, No. 3 on gray stone washed paper, No. 4 on light brown patch paper, Nos. 5 & 6 on maroon corduroy paper, Nos. 7 & 8 on dark green corduroy paper, No. 9 on light brown corduroy paper, No. 10 on green shadow paper, Nos. 11, 12, 13 & 14 on green patch paper.

3. Cut all patterns from the designated paper except pattern numbers 10 through 14. Tear around the edges of patterns 10 through 14, or use the decorative edge scissors for a different look.

4. Beginning with number 1, glue pieces in numerical order on top of blue shadow paper.

5. Glue the finished collage to a piece of black shadow paper.

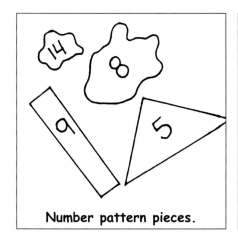

Number pattern pieces.

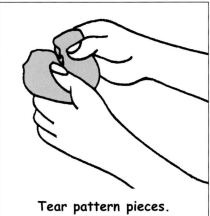

Tear pattern pieces.

Glue pieces in place in numerical order.

Strathmore Kids™ Series Shadow Paper, Patch Paper, Pure Paper Corduroy Paper, Stone Washed Paper, Translucent Vellum; Fiskars® Scissors, Paper Edgers

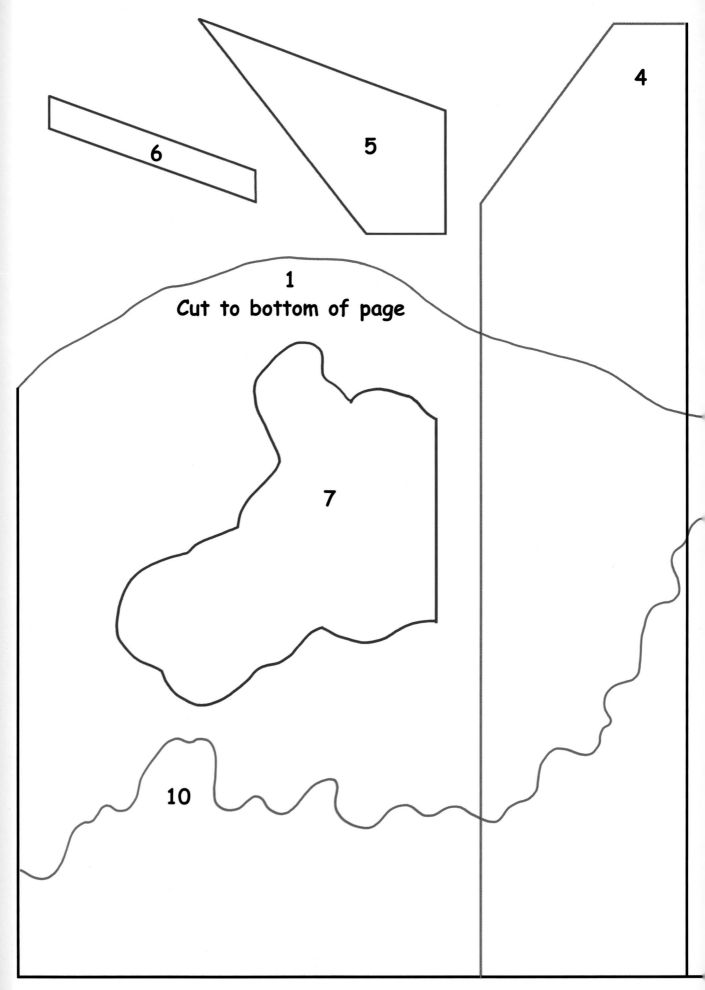

4

6

5

1
Cut to bottom of page

7

10

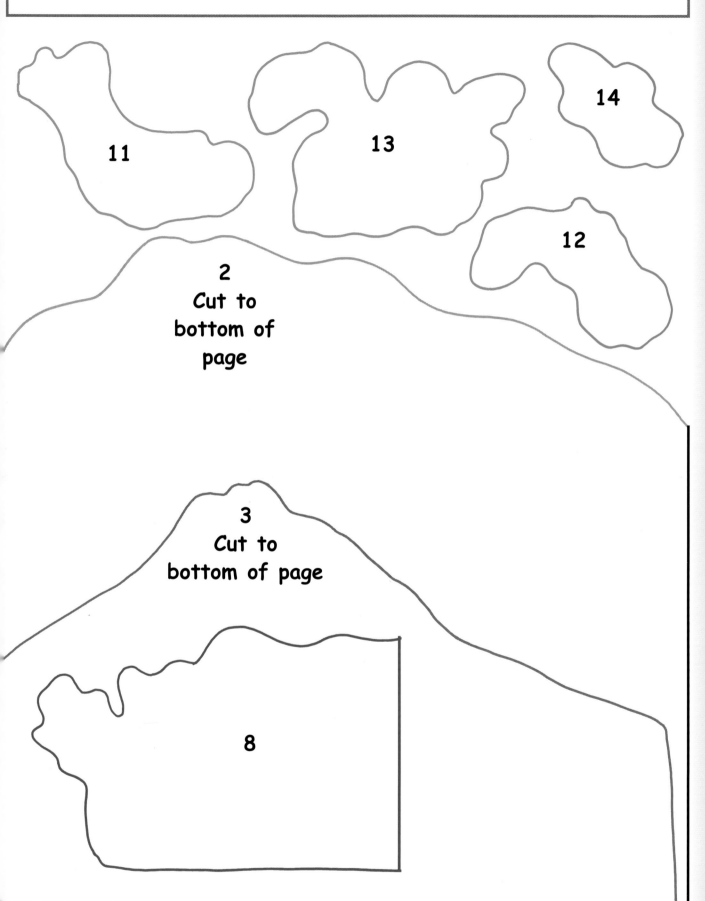

9

11

13

14

12

2
Cut to
bottom of
page

3
Cut to
bottom of page

8

Milano Keys
by Beth Wheeler

Milano silversmiths were known for their intricate lock and key designs.

You will need:
Plastic backed foil sheets - 1 pink,
  1 bright pink, 1 silver
Heart holographic stickers
Cardboard or empty cereal box
22 Gauge craft wire - 4 feet
Assorted beads
Double stick tape
Stylus
Scissors
Permanent marker
Craft snips
Pencil
$1/8$" Hole punch

1. Place heart, key and lock patterns on cardboard. Trace, then cut one of each shape.

2. Crumple pink foil into a ball. Smooth it out gently, leaving some texture.

3. Place large cardboard heart on wrong side of pink foil. Trace around edge with stylus, then cut out $1/2$" larger than traced lines all the way around. Place small cardboard heart on wrong side of bright pink foil. Trace with stylus and cut out $1/2$" larger. Cut lock and key shapes from silver foil in same manner.

4. Wrap foil around cardboard pieces, securing on back with double stick tape.

5. Add details with permanent marker. Add texture to foil shapes with stylus.

6. Position smaller heart on top of the larger one, then attach with double stick tape.

7. Punch holes in large heart and lock as shown on the patterns.

8. Cut two 24" pieces of craft wire with snips. Thread end of one piece of wire through one hole at top of the heart. Twist the end around itself to secure. Thread beads onto the wire, distributing evenly. Wind the wire around a pencil to coil, leaving 1 $1/2$" at the end straight. Thread end of wire through remaining hole at top of the heart. Twist to secure. Adjust the coils as desired.

9. Thread the end of the remaining piece of wire through the hole in the key. Twist to secure. Insert opposite end through the hole at the bottom of the heart and through the hole in the lock. Twist end to secure.

10. Wind the wire around a pencil to coil. Adjust lock and key so one hangs higher than the other.

11. Add heart stickers as desired.

Reynolds® Bright Ideas™ Ultra™ Foil Sheets, Stylus, Double Sided Tape; Toner Plastics, Inc.™ Fun Wire™; Darice® Beads; Fiskars® Scissors, Softouch Craft Snips, Hole Punch;

LOCK PATTERN

Welcome

HEART PATTERN

KEY PATTERN

Millefiori

by Julie McGuffee

This term means "thousands of flowers". It is another name for mosaic beads, where designs and colors are fused together.

You will need:
Clay - white, blue, red, yellow
Small glass jar
Plastic knife
Wax paper
Rolling Pin

1. Knead the clay until soft.

2. Use your hand to roll the red, yellow and white clay into 6" long ropes Start with one yellow rope about ¹/₂" thick, six red ropes about ¹/₄" thick and six white ropes about ¹/₂" thick.

3. Place the white ropes lengthways around the yellow, then the red ones between the white.

4. Roll the blue clay between two pieces of wax paper until it is about 6" long and wide enough to wrap around the group of colored ropes. Wrap around the group of colored ropes.

5. Lay the roll of colors on wax paper, then roll backwards and forwards with your hand, adding pressure up and down the rope until it is about ¹/₂" thick.

6. Use the plastic knife to slice thin pieces off the end of the rope. Starting at the bottom of the glass, push each slice of clay in place around the glass jar.

7. Place on an ovenproof glass in a 275° oven in a well ventilated area. Heat for about 20 minutes. Let cool then remove. DO NOT USE A MICROWAVE OVEN.

Roll clay into ropes.

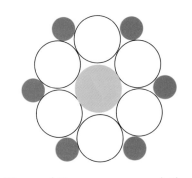

Place white ropes around the yellow, then the red.

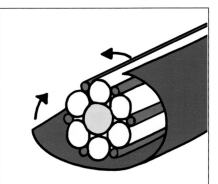

Roll blue clay flat, then wrap around the colored ropes.

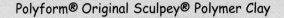

Polyform® Original Sculpey® Polymer Clay

Labyrinth Pendant
by Patty Cox

A Labyrinth is a maze design used as patterns on the floors of many cathedrals. The purpose is to travel the path of the maze as a searching journey to your goal at the center of the maze.

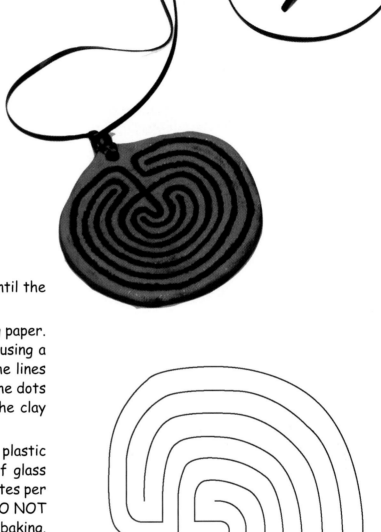

You will need:
2 oz. Copper colored clay
Tracing paper
Black acrylic paint
28" Length black craft lace
4mm Black pony bead
Paint brush
Paper towel
Steel wool
Pencil
Plastic knife

1. Press or roll clay on a flat surface until the clay is smooth.

2. Trace labyrinth pattern onto tracing paper. Transfer traced pattern onto clay by using a pencil point to press tiny dots along the lines of the pattern into the clay. Connect the dots to form pattern line. Form a hole in the clay above the labyrinth with the pencil.

3. Cut around labyrinth and hole with plastic knife. Place labyrinth on an oven proof glass surface, and bake at 275°F for 15 minutes per $1/4$" thickness, with good ventilation. DO NOT USE MICROWAVE OVEN. Avoid over baking. Let cool.

4. Paint black paint and water over labyrinth impression. Wipe away excess paint using a paper towel. Let dry.

5. To shine surface, rub with steel wool.

6. Fold 28" length of black craft lace in half. Insert fold through pendant hole. Tie a lark's head knot. Thread a pony bead on lace. Tie an overhand knot in lace to secure bead over pendant. Tie ends together.

LABYRINTH PATTERN

Polyform Original Sculpey® Polymer Clay; Strathmore Kids™ Series Tracing Paper; Delta Ceramcoat® Acrylic Paint; Toner Plastics, Inc. CraftLace™; Darice® Pony Bead

Abacus

by Leslie Frederick

This is a calculating tool made of rows of beads on a rod. It was invented during the second century B.C., but the first written record was a sketch in the 14th century in the Yuan Dynasty.

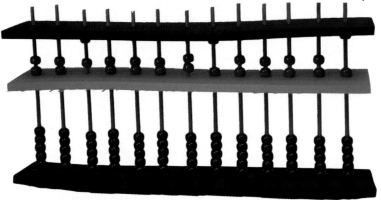

You will need:

6mm Foam sheets - one red, one black
13 Dowels - $1/8$" x 6"
Pony beads - 26 yellow, 65 green
Craft drill with $1/8$" drill bit

White pencil
Scissors
Ruler
Glue
Rubber bands

1. Cut two strips of black foam and one strip of red foam 2" x 9 $1/2$".

2. Draw a line down the center of one strip. Starting $1/4$" from end, make 13 marks along the line 3/4" apart.

3. Place a rubber band around the three strips with the measured foam on top. Place on a hard surface that will not be harmed by the drill. Drill a hole at each mark through all three sheets of foam.

4. Insert a dowel into each hole in the black strip. Place 5 green beads on each dowel. Place the red foam piece onto the dowels, then add 2 yellow beads on each dowel above the red foam. Place the remaining black foam strip on top of the dowels.

5. Lay the Abacus on its side, sliding the beads away from the foam strips. Apply a small dot of glue to each hole. This will secure the foam that forms the framework for the Abacus. Let dry thoroughly before using.

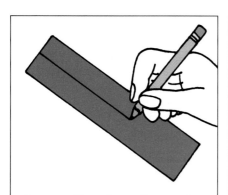

Draw a line down the center of one strip of foam.

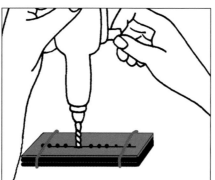

Drill holes in the foam along the center line $3/4$" apart.

Glue the dowels to the holes in the foam.

Darice® Foamies™, Pony Beads; Fiskars® Craft Drill, Scissors, Ruler; Forster® Dowels; Beacon™ Craft Foam Glue™

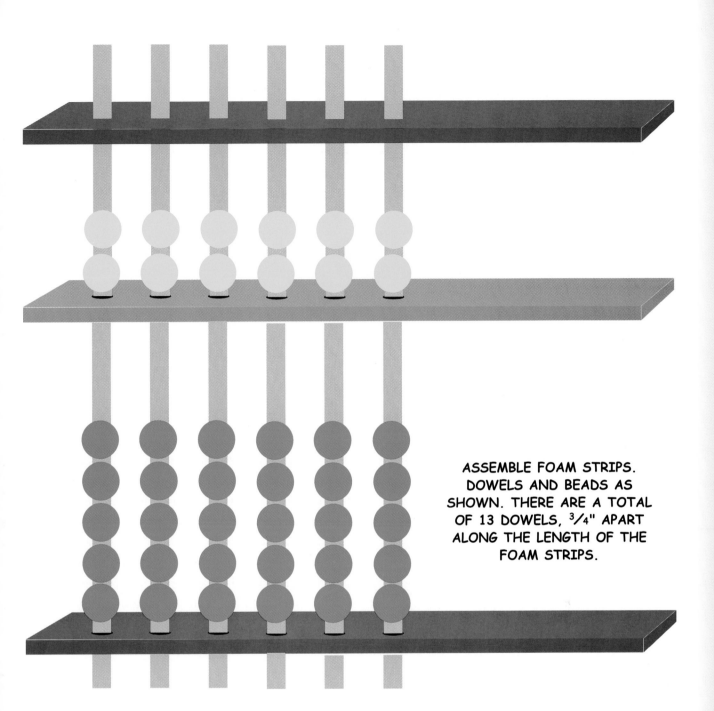

ASSEMBLE FOAM STRIPS. DOWELS AND BEADS AS SHOWN. THERE ARE A TOTAL OF 13 DOWELS, 3/4" APART ALONG THE LENGTH OF THE FOAM STRIPS.

How to use:

Calculations are performed by placing the Abacus flat on a table or on one's lap and manipulating the beads with the fingers on one hand.

Each bead in the *upper deck* has a value of five; each bead in the *lower deck* has a value of one.

Beads are considered counted, when moved *towards* the beam that separates the decks.

The far right column is the "ones" column; the next column to the left is the "tens" column; the next column to the left is the "hundreds"

column, and so on. After 5 beads are counted in the lower deck, the result is "carried" to the upper deck; after both beads in the upper deck are counted, the result (10) is then carried to the next column to the left.

Floating point calculations are performed by designating a space between 2 columns as the decimal point. All the rows to the right of that space represent fractions while all the rows to the left represent whole numbers.

Foam Dragon
by Mary Ayres

The dragon represents wisdom and power in the Chinese culture. It is the imperial symbol of China though the origin is unknown.

You will need:	
Red craft foam	1/8" Circle hand punch
Pony beads - 12 each of purple, blue, green, yellow, orange and red	Fine point black permanent marker
	Pencil
	Glue
4 Yards craft metallic black cord	Scissors

1. Trace, then cut pattern from red craft foam. Press pencil point through pattern at circles to mark placement of holes in foam.

2. Punch 1/8" holes in foam at pencil dots.

3. Draw eye, mouth, nostril and line around the edge of the dragon with black marker.

4. Cut twelve, 10" pieces of black craft cord for beading, and one 7" piece of craft cord for hanger. Apply a dot of glue to each of the cord ends, rubbing the glue and the cord end between your thumb and index finger to form a stiff point.

5. Thread a 10" cord through a hole on the underside of the dragon. Bring cord ends together, then string beads on cord in the following order: purple, blue, green, yellow, orange, red. Knot cord ends together 1" from the ends. Repeat for each hole on underside of dragon.

6. Trim cord ends to 1/2" past knots. Insert ends of 7" cord into holes in top side of dragon, going from front to back. Knot ends of the cord at the back.

Draw a eye, mouth and nostrils with black marker.

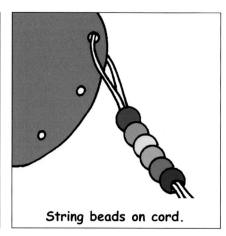
String beads on cord.

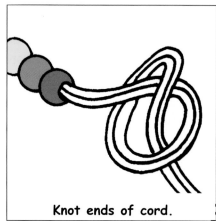
Knot ends of cord.

Darice® Foamies™, Pony Beads, Bright Jewel Metallic Cord; Fiskars® Hand Punch, Scissors; Beacon™ Kids Choice Glue™

DRAGON PATTERN

Terra Cotta Picture Frame

by Sandy Laipply

Terra Cotta was used extensively in China. This project is in honor of the Terra Cotta soldiers of the tomb of the emperor of the Qin Dynasty 221-206 B.C. Chinese Terra Cotta vases have been discovered from as early as 3000 B.C.

You will need:
5" x 7" Wooden frame
1.75 lb. box Terra Cotta clay
Brown acrylic paint
Faux finish glaze
Matte varnish
Sealer
Chinese character stamp
Paintbrush
Glue
Plastic knife
Scissors
Rolling pin

1. Carefully remove glass from wood frame and set aside. Mask the inside and outer edges of frame with tape, if desired. Paint a thin coat of glue over remaining surface. Allow to dry. Remove tape.

2. Knead clay till soft and smooth then roll out to about 1/4" thick with rolling pin. Using a plastic knife, cut strips of flattened clay the width of frame. Lay pieces on the front until the entire frame is covered. Blend seams together with fingers.

3. Use scissors to cut rubber stamps apart into individual Chinese characters. Push different stamps into the clay making sure they leave an impression. Character patterns can be place in rows or in a random fashion. **Option**: Draw Chinese characters on clay with pencil.

4. Place clay covered frame on an oven proof glass surface then bake in a 275°F oven for 15 minutes per 1/4" of thickness, with good ventilation. **DO NOT USE MICROWAVE OVEN.**

Avoid over baking. Thicker pieces may require additional baking time. Let cool.

5. Paint the surface of the frame with a coat of sealer. Let dry.

6. Mix equal parts brown paint and clear glaze. Brush this mixture over entire frame making sure to get into all crevices. Immediately wipe with a paper towel, removing as much color as desired. Let dry.

7. To finish, apply 2 coats of matte varnish, allowing to dry between coats.

Push stamps into to clay to make an impression.

Polyform Original Sculpey® Polymer Clay; Darice® Wood Frame; Delta Ceramcoat® Acrylic Paint, All Purpose Sealer, Faux Finish Glaze, Matte Interior Varnish, Rubber Stampede® Stamp; Beacon™ Gem-Tac™ Glue; Fiskars® Scissors

Tetrahedron Kite

by Sandi Genovese

The Chinese were the first people ever to make and fly kites. Some were designed as animals and many were very large. National kite flying day in China is in April.

You will need:
Die-cut machine or
  pattern and scissors
Die - Kite, Tetrahedron 3-D
Red tissue paper
Background stamp
Black stamp pad
Straws
String
Adhesive

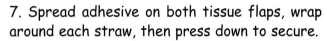

ASSEMBLE THE FRAME

1. Cut 4 strings 3' long and 8 strings 2' long.

2. Thread one of the 3' strings through 3 straws (each straw should be 7 ¾" long). Tie the ends so that you create a triangle with the straws. Tie double knots for strength. Do not cut off the excess string.

3. Tie one of the 2' lengths of string to one of the triangle joints. Thread the string through two straws, then pull them around to create a rhombus. Tie securely.

4. Tie one 2' string at each joint of the opposing corners of the rhombus. Thread one of the strings through a straw, pull it up and tie a double knot to form the 3-D tetrahedron shape.

COVER THE FRAME

5. You will need four folded tissue shapes to cover the assembled frames. Rubber stamp the black ink design on the red tissue. When using the die to cut the tissue, first fold the tissue in half. Place the folded edge on the die where the cutting blade stops. It helps to place a strip of masking tape on the rubber side of the die to act as a guide for paper placement. Trim any excess tissue from the sides before placing in machine and cutting.

6. Open the tissue, then place adhesive in the seam along the fold. Place the tetrahedron on the tissue with one straw on top of the fold.

7. Spread adhesive on both tissue flaps, wrap around each straw, then press down to secure.

8. Rotate the tetrahedron so that the straw triangle sits on the remaining tissue. Spread adhesive on both tissue flaps. Wrap the flaps around each straw, then press down. (Only two faces of each tetrahedron are covered.) Repeat steps 2–8 three times. You will need 4 tissue covered tetrahedrons to make one kite.

COMPLETE THE KITE ASSEMBLY

9. Place two of the tetrahedrons (A and B) side by side with the open or uncovered face of the tetrahedron on the bottom. Use the loose strings at the joints to tie the two together.

10. Place the third tetrahedron (C) behind the first two with open face down, then tie the two together.

11. Attach the final tetrahedron (D) to the top of A, B, and C. Make certain that all the knots are tied securely to prevent the kite from coming apart in the air.

12. To complete the kite, attach the guide string. The best position for this is along the back spine, or you may experiment by tying in different places.

ASSEMBLE THE FRAME

Thread one, 3' string through 3 straws. Knot ends.

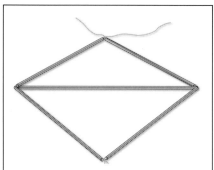

Attach 2' string. Thread through 2 straws, then tie.

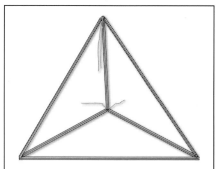

Thread 2' string through straw. Attach points together.

COVER THE FRAME

Place a strip of masking tape along fold line on top of die.

Place folded tissue paper on die with fold against tape.

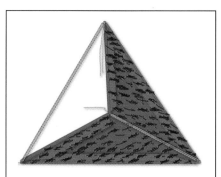

Glue straw to fold. Cover two triangle areas of frame only.

ASSEMBLE THE KITE

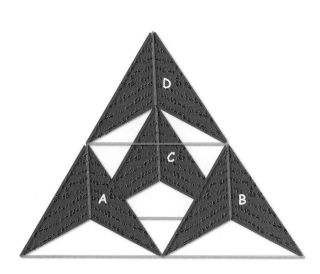

Following steps 9 - 11, use strings to tie tetrahedrons together.

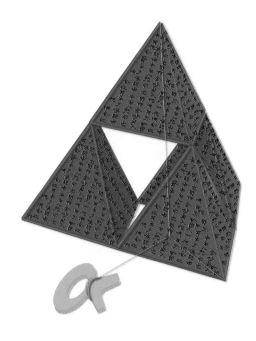

Attach the guide string to the back spine.

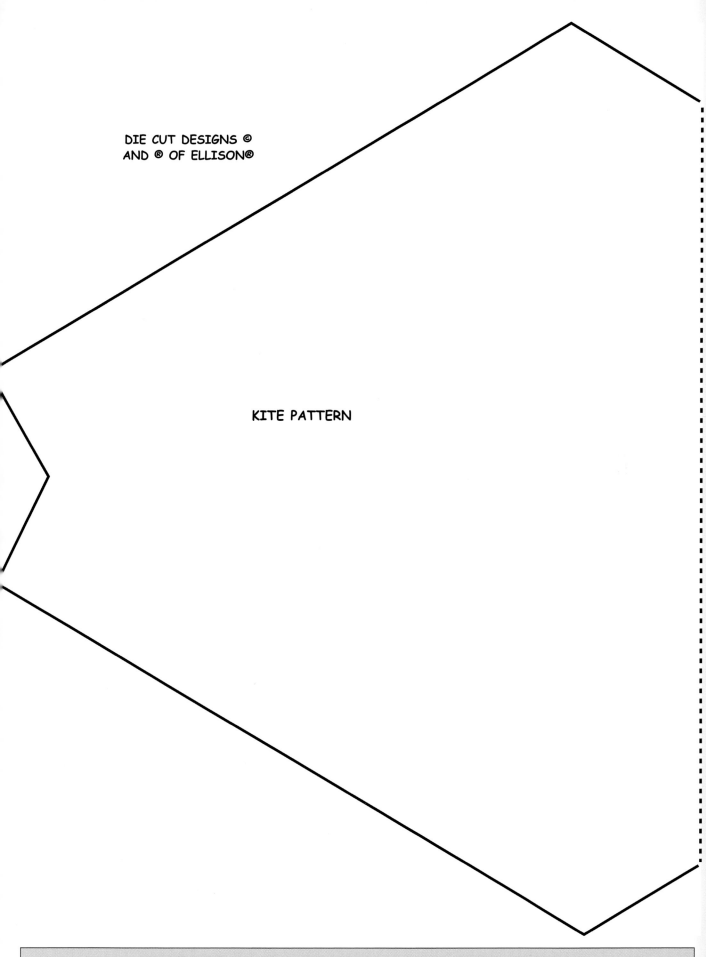

DIE CUT DESIGNS ©
AND ® OF ELLISON®

KITE PATTERN

Ellison® XL Ellison® Letter Machine™, Instructional and Decorative Dies

Symbolic Book Cover

by Cheryl Ball

Chinese calligraphy is an art form over 2000 years old that remains basically unchanged. Lines and brush strokes represent words and letters.

You will need:

Acrylic paint - black, metallic gold
Foam Chinese character stamp
Wood handle Chinese character stamp
8 1/2" x 11" Red vellum
8 1/2" x 11" Craft paper -
  3 black, 1 metallic gold
8 - 10 sheets 5" x 8" ivory craft paper
Decorative edge scissors
Two pieces 5 3/4" x 8 3/4" lightweight
  cardboard

Yard black ribbon - 1/2" wide
Gold button with shank
Small black tassel
Bamboo skewer
Stencil sponges
Scissors
1/4" Hole punch
Double stick tape
Double stick foam tape
Ruler

Delta Ceramcoat® Acrylic Paint, Rubber Stampede® Decorative Stamp, Stencil Sponges;
Strathmore Bright Translucent Vellum, Craft Paper, Reflections Paper;
Fiskars® Paper Edgers, Scissors, Ruler, Hole Punch

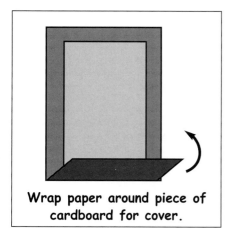

Wrap paper around piece of cardboard for cover.

Thread ribbon through book cover and inside pages.

Tie skewer to side of book with ends of ribbon.

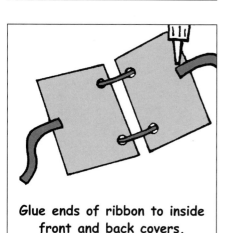

Glue ends of ribbon to inside front and back covers.

1. To make the cover for the book, place a piece of cardboard on top of a sheet of black paper. Wrap the edges of the paper to the back, just like wrapping a present. Use the double stick tape to hold in place. Cut a separate sheet from the black paper a little smaller than the cover. This will be for the inside front cover. Repeat to make back cover. Set aside.

2. Tear a narrow strip off one of the long sides of the red vellum. Measure over about 5", then tear again. This will be the paper for the front of the book. Squeeze out gold metallic paint onto a plate. Dip the flat end of a stencil sponge in the paint, tapping off any excess paint. Lightly sponge the paint onto the wood handled Chinese character stamp. Apply a thin even coat. Stamp the design onto the red vellum using even pressure. Carefully lift the stamp. Apply more paint and continue to randomly stamp on the red vellum. Refer to photo for placement. Let dry.

3. Cut a five inch square of the gold metallic paper. Squeeze black paint onto a plate. Dip flat end of a stencil sponge into paint, tapping off excess. Apply an even coat of paint to the raised design on the foam stamp. Press firmly on the metallic paper, being careful not to let the stamp slip on the shiny paper. Carefully lift the stamp. Let dry. Using the decorative edge scissors, trim the paper to $1/2$" around design.

4. Punch three holes down one side of the cover. Using this as a pattern for placement, punch holes in all filler pages and back cover.

5. Position the vellum paper on the black front cover. Fold any excess to the back, then tape in place. Tape the inside front cover paper in place. Cut 4 one inch squares of foam tape. Peel off backing and press one square onto each corner of the metallic gold square at the back. Press gold square in place on the front cover.

6. Cut four, 10" pieces of ribbon. Assemble the book, front cover, filler pages, and back cover. Thread one piece of ribbon into each hole passing through all the layers of the book. Secure with a knot. Lay the skewer next to the knots, then tie another knot around the skewer to hold it in place. Trim ends.

7. To tie the book closed, cut the remaining piece of ribbon in half. Glue one piece to the front inside cover and one to the back. Let dry. Glue the button to the front, then hang the tassel from the button.

Emperor's Coin
by Patty Cox

This pendant is a replica of a coin from the Ming Dynasty.

SAMPLES OF CHINESE CHARACTERS

福　　健康　　喜

You will need:
2oz. Package Terra Cotta clay
28" Length black craft lace
Disk bead
Pony bead
Plastic knife
Toothpick

1. Knead the clay till soft and smooth. Roll into a $3/4$" ball of clay. Using fingers, press ball into the shape of a 1 $3/8$" disk, about $1/8$" thick. Mark the center of the coin with a dot.

2. Cut out a small square, about $3/8$", in center of coin with a plastic knife.

3. Mark Chinese characters around edges with the toothpick.

4. Bake on an oven proof glass surface at 275°F for 15 minutes per $1/4$" of thickness, with good ventilation. DO NOT USE MICROWAVE OVEN. Avoid over baking. Thicker pieces may require additional baking time. Let cool.

5. Fold craft lace in half. Insert fold through center of coin. Tie a lark's head knot. Thread a disk bead and a pony bead on lace. Tie an overhand knot securing the beads over coin. Tie lace ends together for necklace.

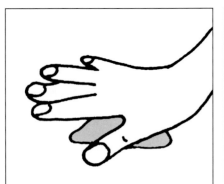

Press ball of clay into the shape of a disk.

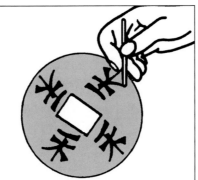

Mark Chinese characters around edge with toothpick.

Thread beads on lace. Secure with overhand knot.

Polyform Original Sculpey® Polymer Clay; Darice® Disk Bead, Pony Bead; Toner Plastics, Inc.™ Craft Lace™

Tag Bag

by Leslie Frederick

Treasured items were often carried in animal skin bags. This bag also doubles as a "memo" pad.

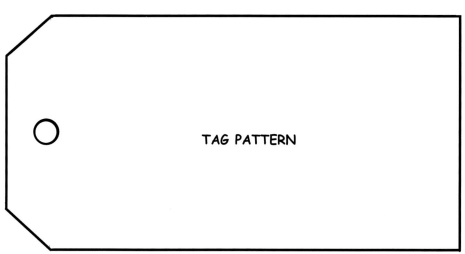

You will need:
2mm Tan foam sheet
Assorted pony beads
Decorative edge scissors
1/8" Hole punch
54" Plastic craft lace - any 2 colors,
58" Plastic craft lace - third color
Assorted colored markers
Paper manila tags, or manila folder
Ruler
Scissors

1. Cut one 4" x 9" strip of foam. Trim edges with decorative edge scissors.

2. Referring to design, decorate foam with the colored markers.

3. Fold foam strip in half for the book cover. Punch a hole at the center of the fold.

4. Trim manila tags to 4" lengths, or cut your own from a manila folder using pattern as a guide. Punch a hole in the center of each one at the top.

5. Slide the tags inside foam, aligning the holes. Thread a 4" piece of craft lace through the holes. Add beads for decoration, then knot the lace to secure.

6. Braid three pieces of different colored craft lace together. Knot ends. Slip the tag book over the braided belt and tie around your waist.

Optional: Punch a hole in the open end of the book. Tie a small piece of craft lace through the holes to keep your tag book closed.

Fold foam in half to make the cover.

TAG PATTERN

Darice® Foamie™, Pony Beads; Fiskars® Paper Edgers, Hole Punch, Scissors; Toner Plastics, Inc.™ CraftLace™

NATIVE AMERICAN NORTH AMERICA

Wampum Necklace

by Dimples Mucherino

The color of the beads symbolized different things. White symbolized health, peace and riches; purple - sympathy and sorrow. Dark purple was the most valuable.

You will need:
White polymer clay
Satin glaze
Acrylic paint - ivory, aqua,
   black, gold, red, blue
Three 11" lengths 22 gauge
   craft wire
Three 30" lengths #20
   hemp cord
$3/16$" x 12" Wood dowel
4 Craft picks
Styrofoam disk
Paint brushes
Needle nose pliers
Scissors
Ruler
Old toothbrush

1. Knead clay till soft and smooth. Divide into one - 1" and four - $1/2$" balls. Flatten the 1" ball to 1" x 2" x $3/8$" thick. Shape with fingers into an arrowhead, pressing fingers into sides to make upper indentation. Flatten and taper side edges. Roll each $1/2$" ball into a wampum bead. Poke one craft pick through the center of each bead. Turn gently to smooth and form hole.

2. Bake clay pieces on an oven proof glass at 275°F for 15 minutes per $1/4$" thickness, with good ventilation. DO NOT USE MICROWAVE OVEN. Avoid over baking. Let cool.

3. Paint the clay pieces as follows: 2 beads gold, 2 beads red and the arrowhead aqua.

Hint: Place bead on a craft pick, then paint the bead. Push opposite end of pick into styrofoam. Let dry.

4. Spatter all pieces with ivory paint by dipping tips of old toothbrush into paint. Hold brush 6" from object, then pull a craft stick across the top of the bristles <u>towards you</u> to spatter paint. Repeat with black. Let dry then coat with glaze.

5. Fold one 11" piece of wire in half. Twist together several times below fold making a small loop in center. Center loop on top back of arrowhead with ends extending to opposite sides. Wrap each end in opposite directions around indentation, then twist together on back. Continue wrapping wire in opposite directions, folding ends to back. Make wire beads by wrapping each remaining wire in tight coil around dowel. Remove from dowel. Set aside.

6. Align lengths of hemp cord. Tie one end together in a knot. Braid strands to opposite end. Tie end in small knot.

7. String beads and arrowhead as pictured. Knot ends of braid together, then trim.

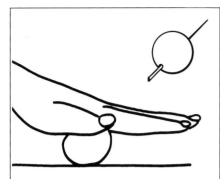

Roll each clay ball into a
Wampum bead. Push onto pick.

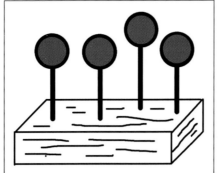

Push ends of craft picks into
Styrofoam until paint dries.

Run finger or craft stick over
toothbrush bristles to spatter
paint over clay pieces.

Fold wire in half, then twist
ends together to make loop.

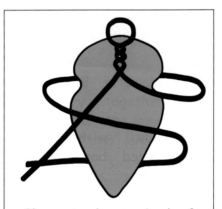

Place wire loop on back of
Wampum. Wrap ends around.

Wrap wire around pendant,
crossing at front.

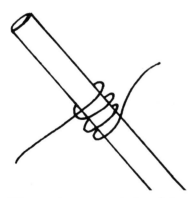

Wrap wire around dowel to
make wire beads.

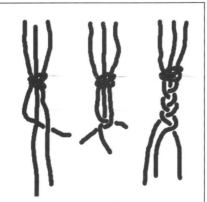

Braid jute to make the cord
for necklace.

Thread clay and wire beads
onto braided jute.

NATIVE AMERICAN NORTH AMERICA

Polyform® Original Sculpey® Polymer Clay, Glaze; Delta Ceramcoat® Acrylic Paint; Toner Plastics, Inc.™
Fun Wire™; Darice® Hemp Cord; Forster® Wood Dowels, Craft Picks;
Fiskars® Micro-Tip® Needle Nose Pliers, Scissors, Ruler

Hogan Box
by Patty Cox

The Navaho Hogan is an eight sided structure made of logs. The female Hogan is the family home where children are raised. A smaller structure where men meet, is the male Hogan. The door of the Hogan always faces east to meet the rising sun.

You will need:
Mini craft sticks, colored or natural
3/4" Wooden cube
6" x 6" x 1/8" Balsa wood, or
  6" x 6" piece of cardboard
Glue
Ruler
Sharp edge or craft knife
Optional: 1 1/2" Square of leather

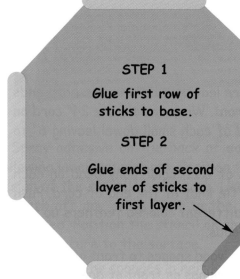

STEP 1

Glue first row of sticks to base.

STEP 2

Glue ends of second layer of sticks to first layer.

STEP 3

Bring sticks 1/8" closer together when layering to form the lid.

1. Using pattern, cut a 5 3/4 " octagon from balsa wood with a craft knife and ruler. For younger crafters, the hogan base can be cut from poster board or cardboard.

2. Glue a mini craft stick to the base at the top, bottom and each side (Step 1). Apply glue to ends of four craft sticks, then place craft sticks across the diagonal corners of the octagon (Step 2). Continue layering until there are 16 levels for walls.

3. To make the box lid, lay 4 craft sticks on top of wall sides. <u>DO NOT GLUE</u>. Apply glue on top of the ends of each craft stick, then place the ends of an additional 4 craft sticks on glue in diagonal corners of the octagon (Step 3). With each new level, bring craft sticks in about 1/8" toward center of box to form the dome roof. Continue layering until there are 16 levels to form a domed roof.

4. Glue about 13 craft sticks across the top layer of the roof to cover the top.

5. Glue a 3/4" wooden cube at the center of the top of the box for the chimney handle.

6. **Optional:** Fold 1 1/2" square of leather in half. Glue between box bottom and lid for hinge. Glue and tuck leather ends between craft sticks.

Darice® Mini Craft Sticks, Wood Cube, Leather; Midwest Products Co.,Inc. Micro-Cut® Quality Wood; Beacon™ Kids Choice Glue™; Fiskars® Ruler

Denim Rug

by Cheryl Ball

Apples are a traditional colonial design. Only wealthy people had rugs, others made painted rugs of canvas from ship's sails.

You will need:
Old jeans
Acrylic paint - red, green, white
Square checkerboard rubber stamp
Fruit stencil
Stencil sponge
Scissors
Clothespins
Cotton swabs
Washable glue or sewing machine

1. Cut jeans apart. We will use the pockets, legs, and waist bands. Arrange the pieces on the floor. Add pockets at angles for an interesting design. Use the seams of the jeans and the waist bands for the outside edges for a more finished look. Overlap pieces about an inch. Fold under any cut edges and then glue around the outside, using clothespins to hold edges until dry. Glue or sew all the pieces together to form the rug. Refer to photo for placement.

2. Paint the checkerboard design first, then the apples. Squeeze white paint onto a plate. Dip the flat end of a stencil sponge into the paint, tapping off any excess paint. Lightly sponge an even coat of white paint onto the stamp design, using a pouncing motion. This will evenly distribute the paint on the stamp. Position stamp in place on the surface, then press firmly on the back of the stamp. Carefully lift the stamp. For different looks from the same stamp, apply paint to only certain areas of the stamp, corners, triangles, or squares. Continue adding stamped checks in desired areas. Change paint color, and add red checker boards if desired.

3. To stencil the apples, squeeze red, green and white paint onto a plate. Cut one of the stencil sponges in half lengthwise, then in half again. This will create a smaller sponge for smaller areas. Position the apple stencil on the rug, then press to secure. Dip the flat end of a sponge into red paint, then pounce onto the stencil, filling in the areas evenly. Dip one of the smaller sponge pieces into the green paint, then pounce on the leaves and stem. Pounce a small amount of white paint on one side of the apple to add the highlight.

4. Dip cotton swabs into paint, then use to add red and white dots to sections of the rug where desired. Simply press the swab on surface, adding more paint for each dot.

Delta Ceramcoat® Acrylic Paint, Stencil Mania™, Stencil Sponges, Stencil Magic® Adhesive Spray, Rubber Stampede® Design Element; Fiskars® Scissors

COLONIAL AMERICA

Silver Tray

by Beth Wheeler

Almost every Colonial town had a silversmith who made candlesticks, platters, and bowls. Intricate designs were cut into the metal by engraving.

You will need:
2 Sheets silver, plastic backed foil
Stylus
Double stick tape
Thick white glue
Scissors
Clean plastic foam meat tray
22 Gauge craft wire
Craft snips
Embossing cream

1. Photocopy the pattern provided, enlarging or reducing as necessary to fit on the bottom of your meat tray. Trim excess paper, so just the design remains.

2. Apply double stick tape to the back of the pattern, along edges, but don't remove the backing at this time.

3. Squeeze glue along the pattern lines and dots directly on the paper. Squeeze evenly spaced dots of glue along the lip of the meat tray. Allow the glue to dry completely.

4. Remove backing from pieces of tape, then press paper onto the meat tray surface.

5. Cover the meat tray with silver foil, smoothing it over the glue shapes with your fingers and wrapping the excess over the edges to the back of the tray. Secure to the back with double stick tape. Cut silver foil just large enough to cover the back of the tray. Secure with double stick tape.

6. Emboss around the glue shapes with the stylus for added dimension.

7. Highlight dimensional areas of design by rubbing cream over the ridges with your finger.

8. Twist wire around the tray edges to create handles, twisting ends tightly to secure. Push ends through ends of tray. Trim excess wire from ends with craft snips.

Squeeze glue along the
pattern lines.

Cover the tray with foil.
Secure to back with tape.

Make handles by twisting wire
around the edges.

Reynolds® Bright Ideas™ Ultra™ Foil Sheets, Stylus, Double Sided Tape; Toner Plastics, Inc.™ Fun Wire™;
Fiskars® Softouch Craft Snips, Scissors; Craf-T Products Embossing Cream

SILVER TRAY PATTERN

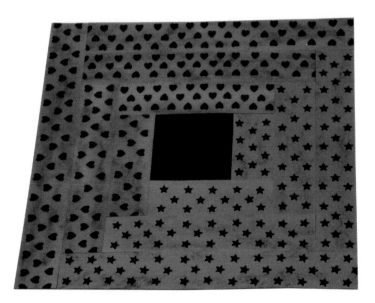

Log Cabin Quilt
by Kathi Taylor Shearer

Not a scrap of fabric was thrown away and patchwork was a common design in Colonial America. This particular pattern looked like stacked logs.

You will need:
Black construction paper
Shadow paper - red, blue
Paper trimmer
Glue stick
Hand punches - heart, star
Ruler
Pencil
Scissors

LOG QUILT PLACEMENT DIAGRAM
(DIAGRAM IS 50% OF ACTUAL SIZE)
FIRST NUMBER INDICATES ORDER OF PLACEMENT
SECOND NUMBER INDICATES THE LENGTH

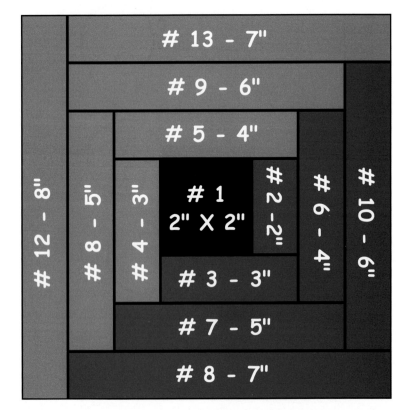

1. Cut an 8" x 8" square and a 2" x 2" square of black construction paper.

2. Using a paper trimmer, or scissors and ruler, cut 1" strips of red and blue shadow paper. Cut the strips as shown on the chart. Punch hearts and star shapes from the strips at this point so black background will show through, or wait until step 5.

3. Use a ruler to mark the middle of the 8" black square. Glue the 2" square to the middle of the 8" square. The 2" square will be your guide for placing the paper strips.

4. Refer to the chart for placement of strips. Glue each strip before you add the next strip. Continue adding strips until the quilt square is complete. Trim black outside edges if necessary.

5. Punch hearts and stars from scraps of paper, then glue to strips to create "fabric" design.

Strathmore Kids™ Series Construction Paper, Shadow Paper; Fiskars® Scissors, Paper Trimmer, Hand Punches, Ruler

Bumble Bee Tassel

by Dorris Sorensen

America was known for simple toys and decorative wood carvings. This tassel holder was a way to add a decorative touch to the home using left-over yarn scraps.

You will need:
Wood tassel topper
18 Gauge wire - black
Acrylic paint - yellow, pink,
  black and white
Plastic lacing - yellow
Compressed sponge
Black permanent marker
Needle nose pliers
Scissors
Varnish
Paintbrush - liner, flat
Glue

1. Paint the tassel topper yellow. Paint a "V" shaped hood with black paint. Paint bottom ring of the topper black. Let dry.

2. Using a small piece of compressed sponge, sponge cheeks on with pink paint. Use a black marker to paint the eyes. Add a tiny white sparkle dot to the cheeks and eyes with the end of paint brush. Add the nose and mouth with black marker.

3. Cut a small piece of sponge about $1/4$" wide. Dip in black paint and sponge on stripes around the body.

4. Paint vertical stripes with yellow paint around black base.

5. Apply one coat of varnish to entire tassel topper. Let dry.

6. Cut two pieces of black craft wire approximately 24" long. Starting with a small loop, work the wire around in a circle with your fingers to form wings. Refer to photo. Glue wings in place.

7. Cut two pieces of black wire about $3 1/2$" long to form antennae. Slightly curl each piece of wire at the top. Glue into the top of the head.

8. To make the tassel, wind yellow craft lace around a piece of cardboard about $5 1/2$" x 4". Wrap lacing around the long way. Wrap as much lacing as you want in your tassel, then tie at the top. Work the lacing off the cardboard and cut at the bottom. Pull tassel up inside the topper and glue in place. Trim the bottom of the lacing to even it up.

Paint the "V" shaped hood and face on tassel top.

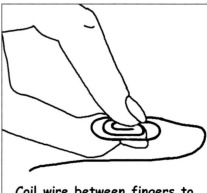

Coil wire between fingers to form spirals for wings.

COLONIAL AMERICA

Zoetrope

by Sandi Genovese

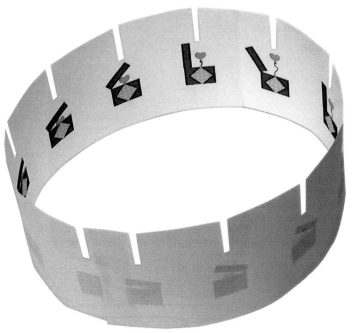

A Zoetrope is a revolving drum with slits on the side. On the inside of the drum is a flexible card with a sequence of 20 - 30 pictures. As you turn the drum and look through the slits, it appears as if the object is moving. This was an early form of motion pictures.

You will need:
Die-cut machine or pattern
   and scissors
Zoetrope die
White construction paper
Colored pens/pencils
Lazy Susan or turntable
Tape

1. Cut two strips to make one Zoetrope.

2. Tape two strips together to make one long strip with a total of twelve slits.

3. Draw your design under each slit, making a slight change in each drawing.

4. When the drawings are complete, tape the ends of the strip together to make what will look like a "crown".

5. Place the "crown" on your Lazy Susan, or turntable. Bend down and look through the slits to see the action come to life.

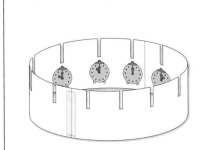

It is best to choose a subject whose motion is continuous—for example, a clock with hands. The twelfth drawing should naturally connect to the first, or use the first six frames to create the action and the last six frames to reverse it. Drawings #1 and #12 will automatically connect when taped together.

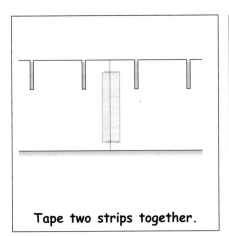

Tape two strips together.

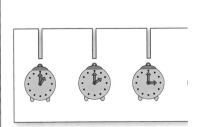

Draw a simple design below each slip.

Tape strip into a circle with design on the inside.

Ellison® XL Ellison® Letter Machine™, Instructional and Decorative Dies;
Strathmore Construction Paper

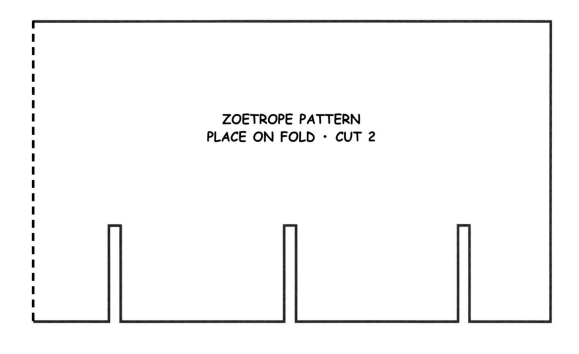

ZOETROPE PATTERN
PLACE ON FOLD · CUT 2

DIE CUT DESIGNS ©
AND ® OF ELLISON®

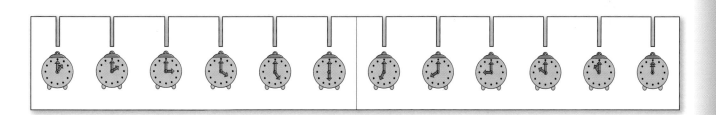

SAMPLE PATTERNS

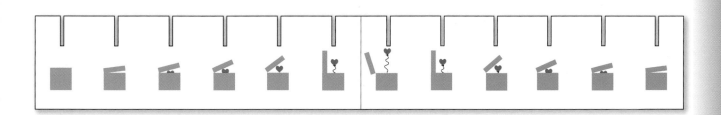

Cotton Bags

by Barbara Matthiessen

The beginning of the Industrial Revolution was based on the cotton industry. Many of the inventions were made for manufacturing and producing cotton.

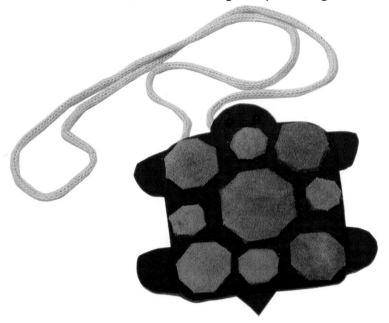

1. Trace, then cut patterns for turtle. Trace patterns onto the back of leather with chalk. Trace body on green leather, shell on brown leather and one large, 4 medium, and 4 small spots onto beige leather. Cut out all pieces just inside the chalk lines.

2. Place wax paper inside purse to prevent glue from seeping through. Spread glue over one side of the purse with a toothpick. Place and press the turtle body in place on the purse with the head at the top. Glue the shell on the back of the turtle so legs, head and tail show evenly on all sides.

Hint: It is easier to spread glue on the upper (smooth) side of the leather when gluing one piece of leather on top of another.

3. Glue large spot to center of shell and medium spots at each corner. Glue small spots between medium spots. Apply dots of glue with the point of a toothpick to head, then press on half round balls for eyes. Let glue dry thoroughly before using the purse.

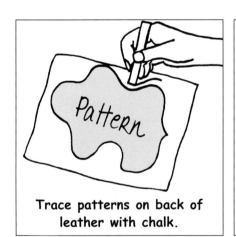

Trace patterns on back of leather with chalk.

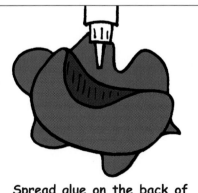

Spread glue on the back of turtle, then glue shell on top.

Apply dots of glue with a toothpick. Press eye in place.

TURTLE PATTERNS

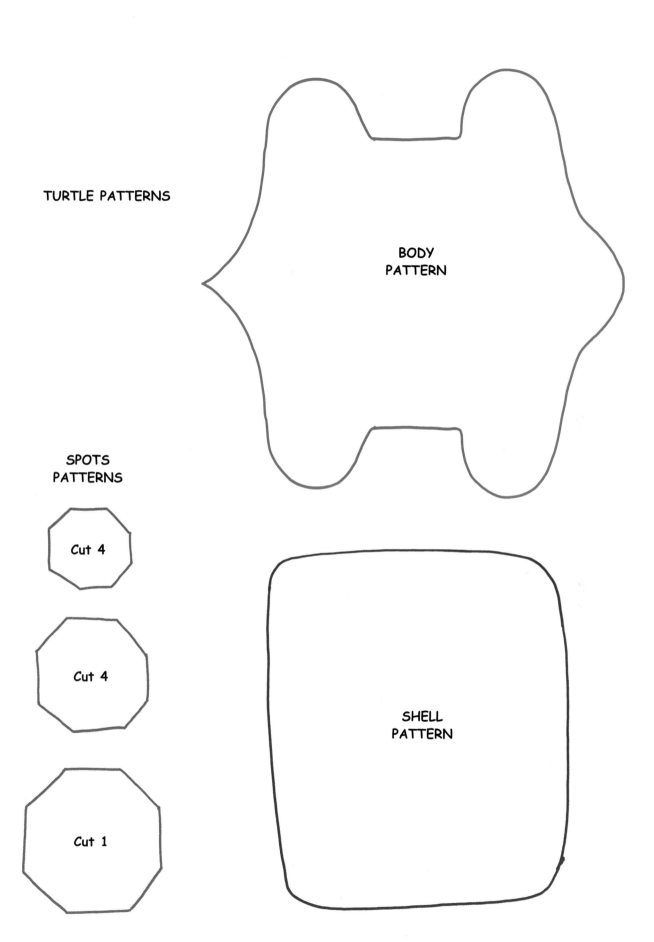

BODY
PATTERN

SPOTS
PATTERNS

Cut 4

Cut 4

Cut 1

SHELL
PATTERN

Sandpaper Pointillism
by Sandi Genovese

Part of the Industrial Revolution also involved a revolution of art forms. Pointillism and George Seurat were an important part of the Neo-Impressionist movement.

You will need:
Die-cut machine or
  pattern and scissors
Ellison dies - Orange/Citrus Slice, Apple,
  Pear, Cherries
Sizzix dies - Flower #1, Fun Serif Alphabet
Crayons
80 Grit sandpaper
White cotton napkin
Dowel
Ribbon
Iron

1. Using the die-cut machine or pattern and scissors, cut desired shapes from 80 grit sandpaper. Letters must be cut backwards to read correctly once the process is complete.

2. Color the grit side of the sandpaper heavily with crayons. (Do not use washable crayons.)

3. Arrange shapes to fit your fabric on a large piece of construction paper, crayon side up .

4. Tape shapes in place with double stick tape.

5. Center fabric over shapes, then cover with a press cloth. (This will protect your iron from any crayon that may seep through.)

6. Use a preheated iron on high. Move iron over entire surface for about 15 – 20 seconds .

7. If item is to be laundered, turn fabric inside out and wash with cold water.

8. To make wall hanging, wrap top of napkin over the dowel, then glue to secure. Attach cord at each end to hang.

9. Use this process to decorate T-Shirts, or other fabric items. Don't forget to cut letters out backwards so they will be correct when the process is complete.

Cut shapes from sandpaper.

Color grit side of sandpaper shapes with crayons.

Arrange shapes into design on top of paper.

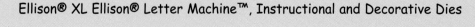
Ellison® XL Ellison® Letter Machine™, Instructional and Decorative Dies

CUT LETTERS BACKWARDS

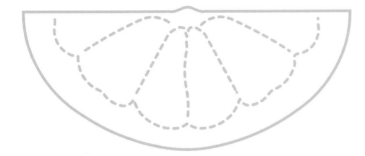

CITRUS SLICE PATTERN

CHERRIES PATTERN

APPLE PATTERN

PEAR PATTERN

INDUSTRIAL REVOLUTION

Wedgwood
by Cheryl Ball

Josiah Wedgwood (1730-1795) revolutionized the production and sale of pottery. Inspired by China ware, Wedgwood was first made during the industrialization of factories using waterwheels to turn machines.

You will need:
Glass paint - white
Glass accent liner - white
Glass surface conditioner
Assorted glass pieces - vases,
    plates, mugs in various colors
Rubber stamps - flower, leaf
Stencil sponges
Scissors
1" Flat paint brush
Cotton swabs

1. Wash and dry the glass pieces.

2. Following instructions on the label, apply surface conditioner to the outside of the glass pieces. Let dry.

3. Squeeze white glass paint on plate. Dip the flat end of a stencil sponge into the paint and tap excess on the plate. Pounce the paint onto the flower design of the foam stamp applying a thin even coat. Position the stamp in place on the glass piece and carefully press. Continue with all flowers and then repeat with the leaf stamp. Refer to photo for placement.

4. The raised look on the design is created with the white accent liner. Start the flow of the paint on a paper towel to practice getting a smooth line. Outline the design first with the accent liner, then using even pressure on the bottle of accent liner, fill in the entire area with a smooth even coat of the paint. Mistakes can be cleaned off with a damp cotton swab. Let the paint dry before adding designs to another side of the glass piece.

5. Let paint dry, and follow label instructions for care of the painted glass pieces.

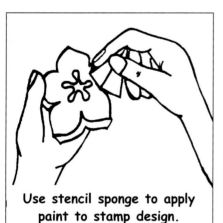

Use stencil sponge to apply paint to stamp design.

Outline the designs with the accent liner.

Use the tip of the accent liner bottle to fill in designs.

Delta Air-Dry PermEnamel™ Paint, Surface Conditioner, Accent Liner, Rubber Stampede® Design Elements, Stencil Sponges; Fiskars® Scissors

Princess Mirror

by Barbara Matthiessen

Modern day mirror making changed with the invention of a new process in 1835.

You will need:

5 ½" x 8" Round hand mirror

18 Gauge gold craft wire

22 Gauge craft wire - gold and green

18mm Red faceted beads

6mm Clear faceted beads

Yarn - any color

Glue

Scissors

Craft snips

Ruler

Cardboard

1. Measure and cut a 3" x 4" and a 12" x 18" piece of cardboard.

2. Wrap yarn around the 3" side of the smaller piece 25 times. Tie off the wrapped yarn with another piece of yarn on one side. Clip the yarn ends on the side opposite then tie to make the bangs. Use the same process wrapping the 12" side of cardboard 40 times to make the rest of the hair.

3. Glue the tied end of the bangs to the center top of the mirror. Apply a line of glue over the top of the bangs and down each side of the mirror frame. Press the tied center of the hair into the glue over the bangs then press the sides of the hair onto the mirror frame. Let dry. Tie sides of hair into pony tails with pieces of yarn. Trim bangs and pony tails with scissors.

4. String 9 clear and 8 red beads onto 18 gauge craft wire starting and ending with a clear bead. Bend a loop at the end of the wire. Starting ½" from the loop, hold onto a clear bead with one hand and base of wire with the other. Twist 2 or 3 times. Continue to the next red bead, bending the wire so that the red bead is about ½" higher than the clear bead, then twist 4 times. Repeat across until all beads are used. Snip the wire from the bundle and curl the end to finish the crown. Place on hair securing wire in back of mirror and glue in place.

5. Have fun adding the finishing touches to your mirror. String more beads on the wire and wrap around pony tails. Use the 22 gauge wire to add additional wraps of gold and green wire to handle. Add beads if desired.

Wrap yarn around cardboard. Tie off then clip ends.

Glue tied ends of bangs to the top of the mirror.

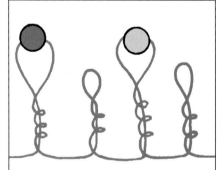

Twist the wire with beads to form the crown.

Toner Plastics, Inc.™ Fun Wire™; Darice® Beads; Fiskars® Scissors, Softouch Craft Snips

Old Glory Fresco
by Patty Cox

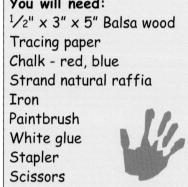

A fresco is a painting on a wall. The fresco technique involves painting on wet plaster. As the plaster dries, it encases the color. The pigments form a permanent bond with the wall. This project involves the same look. The 50th state of the United States was admitted into the Union in 1959.

You will need:
½" x 3" x 5" Balsa wood
Tracing paper
Chalk - red, blue
Strand natural raffia
Iron
Paintbrush
White glue
Stapler
Scissors

1. Squeeze about 1 teaspoon glue on surface of balsa wood. Wet paintbrush in water, then brush glue over one side of board. Add water to brush as needed. Let dry.

2. Tape tracing paper over flag pattern. Color blue area around stars with chalk. The stars don't have to be perfect. Color red stripes with chalk.

3. When glue on board has dried completely, tape flag tracing, chalk side down on board.

4. With adult supervision, iron chalk into glue surface on board. Iron should be set on the wool setting. Move iron over surface about 15-30 seconds. Lift areas of tracing paper to check image. Iron more if needed. Remove tracing paper. The chalk will be permanently bonded into the glue on the wood.

5. Tie a bow in the center of the raffia strand. Knot the two loops to secure bow. Tie overhand knots in each raffia strand, about 3" from bow. Center, then staple raffia to back of balsa wood. Staple above and below knots to secure the raffia hanger. Clip raffia ends.

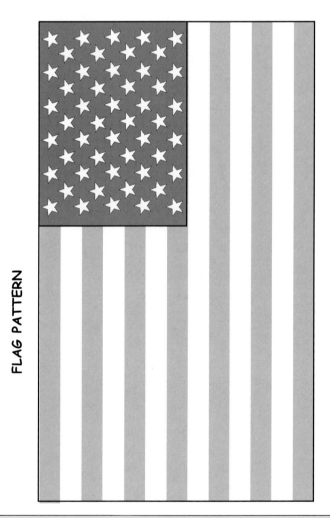

FLAG PATTERN

Midwest Products Co., Inc. Micro-Cut® Quality Woods;
Sakura of America Cray-Pas® Junior Artist Oil Pastels; Darice® Raffia; Fiskars® Scissors

Star Travel Game
by Cheryl Ball

Steam engines, and later railroads, were a big factor in the industrialization of Europe and America. Transportation helped push the world to a time where power driven machinery changed manufacturing.

You will need:
Metal cookie sheet - about 12" x 16"
Acrylic paint - blue, red, yellow
Magnetic sheets
Satin interior varnish
5 Point star stamp (or pattern)
Stencil sponges
Decorative edge scissors
Black permanent marker
1 ½ yds Red jumbo rick rack
2" Square self-stick notes
Glue
Flat paintbrush
Pencil
Scissors
Ruler

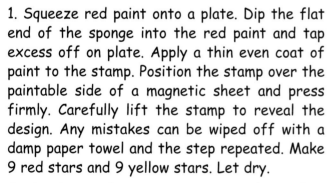

STAR PATTERN

1. Squeeze red paint onto a plate. Dip the flat end of the sponge into the red paint and tap excess off on plate. Apply a thin even coat of paint to the stamp. Position the stamp over the paintable side of a magnetic sheet and press firmly. Carefully lift the stamp to reveal the design. Any mistakes can be wiped off with a damp paper towel and the step repeated. Make 9 red stars and 9 yellow stars. Let dry.

Option: Trace the star pattern onto sheet, then paint red and yellow with paintbrush.

2. Use a flat paintbrush to apply an even coat of the varnish to the stars. Let dry.

3. Outline the stars with black marker. Cut out the stars leaving a little of the white edge showing. Set aside.

4. Cut a piece of the magnetic sheeting to fit the back of the cookie sheet. Trim edges with decorative edge scissors. Use the pencil and ruler to mark off evenly spaced squares on the magnetic sheeting (six 2" squares down and eight 2" squares across).

5. Sponge paint every other square blue. Let first coat dry, then add another. Let dry.

Hint: To ensure that you paint within the lines of the squares, press sheets of self-stick notes around the edges of each square. Remove once paint has dried.

6. Varnish entire surface. Let dry.

7. Glue rick rack around the edge of the pan.

DIE CUT DESIGN © AND ® OF ELLISON®

Delta Ceramcoat® Acrylic Paint, Satin Interior Varnish, Stencil Sponges, Rubber Stampede® Stamp; Fiskars® Scissors, Paper Edgers, Ruler; Darice® Magnetic Sheets

1900's to PRESENT DAY

Art Deco Bulletin Board
by Barb Zimmerman

Art Deco was a popular design movement in the 1920's through the 1930's. One of the most famous examples of Art Deco architecture is the Empire State Building in New York.

You will need:
20" x 30" Foam board
12" Square adhesive backed cork board
Two sheets white patch paper - 9" x 12"
Silver metallic paper
Craft paper - pink, bright blue and purple
Bright green corduroy paper
Decorative edge scissors
Decorative corner edgers
Square hand punch
Scissors
Glue
Ruler
Utility cutter
Pencil

1. Referring to diagram on opposite page, cut the foam board according to dimensions with a utility cutter. This will form the basic shape of your building.

2. Remove adhesive backing from cork board. Place on the foam board 1" from the bottom and 4" from each side.

3. Cut white patch paper into the following pieces to cover first three levels of building:

  Two 1" x 10" pieces for the lower edge,
  Two 4" x 12" pieces for sides of cork board,
  Two 2" x 10" pieces along top of cork board,
  One 3" x 8" piece for 2nd level, and
  One 2" x 6" piece for 3rd level.
Glue these pieces on foam board.

4. Cut one 3" x 4" piece of bright blue craft paper for tower, then glue on foam board.

5. Measure and cut various rectangular sizes of pink, blue and purple craft paper to embellish sides and levels of the building. Refer to picture for ideas. Use corner edgers, decorative edge scissors and a square hand punch to create interesting architectural features. Glue in place. Your Art Deco building should reflect not only the symmetrical and geometric design that is characteristic of the style, but also the use of vibrant colors.

6. Cut the silver metallic paper to create windows for your building. Use strips of the green corduroy paper to help define the windows. Glue in place.

Hint: Place pieces of colored papers on your foam board building to determine placement before gluing. Let dry.

Strathmore Kids™ Series Patch Paper, Pure Paper Corduroy Paper, Brite Hue Paper, Reflections Paper; Fiskars® Scissors, Hand Punch, Paper Edgers, Corner Edgers, Ruler

BULLETIN BOARD DIAGRAM

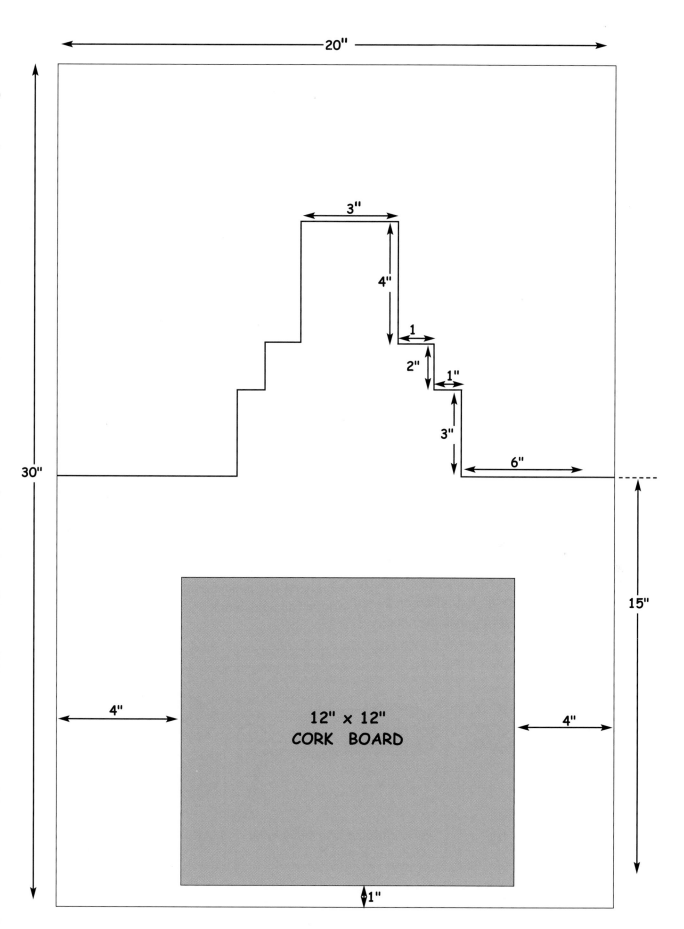

20"

30"

3"

4"

1

2"

1"

3"

6"

15"

4"

12" x 12"
CORK BOARD

4"

1"

Teddy Bear
by Lorine Mason

In 1902, President Teddy Roosevelt lent his name to a plush bear after a story evolved about him not shooting a bear cub, because it could not defend itself. The teddy bear is 100 years old in 2002.

You will need:
Shadow construction paper - brown, yellow
Four ½" metal brads
Polyester stuffing
Two 10mm Wiggle eyes
7mm Brown pom pom
Scissors
Clothespins
⅛" Hole punch
Pencil
Black permanent marker
Glue
Chop stick or pencil
Ribbon
2 Buttons

1. Trace the vest pattern piece onto yellow shadow construction paper and the remaining pattern pieces onto brown. Cut out.

2. Glue the yellow vest onto one of the body sections. On the same body section, glue the small ear pieces onto each ear and the muzzle onto the face. Glue the pairs of body sections (body, arms, and legs) together leaving a small opening in each.

3. Push a small amount of stuffing into the body, arm and leg sections. Use a chop stick or pencil to carefully push the stuffing into corners.

4. Glue the openings together. Use clothespins to hold in place until dry. Remove clothespins.

5. Assemble the bear by punching a hole in shoulders of body and at the top of each arm. Punch a hole in the top of each leg section and at the base of the body. Attach legs and arms to the body with brads so the limbs can move.

6. Glue a ribbon bow and buttons to vest. Glue wiggle eyes and the pom pom nose in place.

7. Using the permanent marker, add a mouth and dots for whiskers.

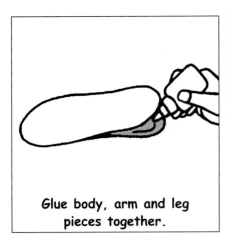

Glue body, arm and leg pieces together.

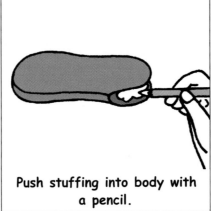

Push stuffing into body with a pencil.

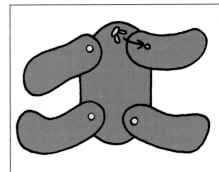

Attach arms and legs to body with brads.

Strathmore Kids™ Series Shadow Paper; Darice® Pom Pom, Wiggle Eyes; Fiskars® Scissors, Hole Punch

TEDDY BEAR PATTERNS

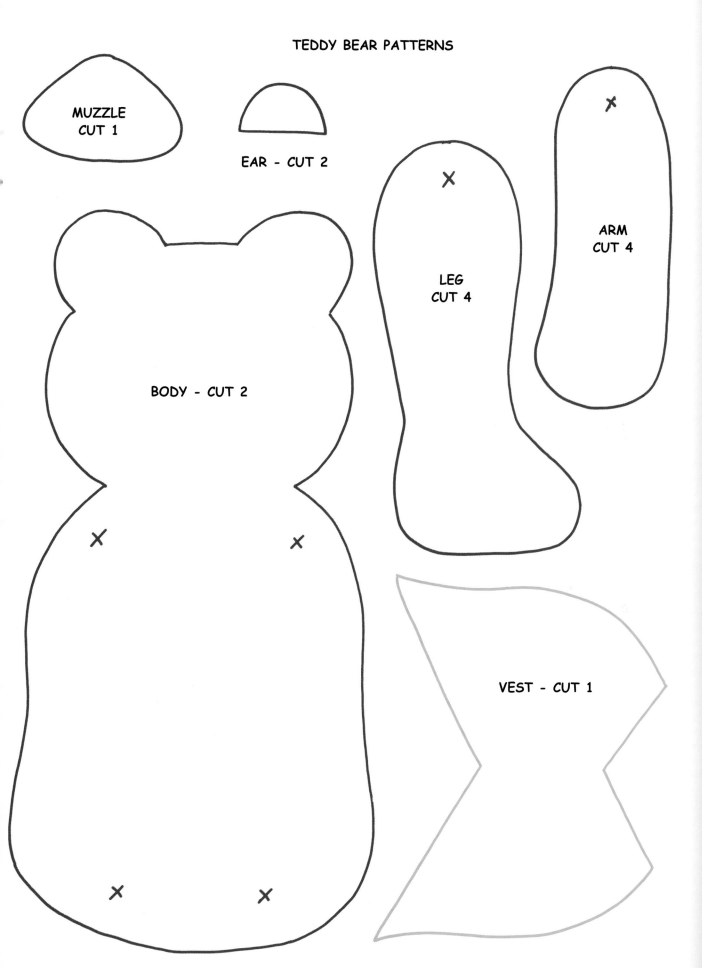

MUZZLE
CUT 1

EAR - CUT 2

ARM
CUT 4

LEG
CUT 4

BODY - CUT 2

VEST - CUT 1

Hologram Bracelet

by Patty Cox

Dennis Gabor invented holography in 1947. He was awarded the Nobel Prize for physics in 1971.

You will need:
7" x 11" Adhesive backed holographic sheet - purple mini radial

Scissors or paper trimmer
12" Length purple embroidery floss
Tablespoon baby powder

1. Cut four, 11" x ¼" strips of holographic foil.

2. Lift paper backing at ends only. Stick lengths end to end, overlapping ends about ¾". Remove all paper backing.

3. Shake baby powder onto a small plate. Slide the adhesive side of strip under your thumb through baby powder. Slide the strip through your fingers to remove excess powder.

4. Bend strip in half to find the center. Fold strip at center with tails at a 90° right angle. Alternate and fold strips over the center until entire strip is folded.

5. Tie off end with a 12" length of embroidery floss. Tie floss around other end.

6. Gently stretch and open folded bracelet.

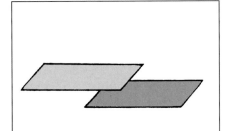

Stick lengths end to end, overlapping about ¾".

Slide adhesive side of strip under thumb through powder.

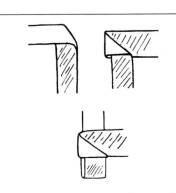

Fold strips at right angles over center.

Reynolds® Bright Ideas™ Holographic Sheets; Fiskars® Scissors, Paper Trimmer

Delta Dart

by Frank Ehling for Midwest Products Co., Inc.

Wilbur and Orville Wright made their historic first flight in 1903.

You will need:
Delta Dart Rubber Powered
 Flying Model Kit #510
Cardboard
Wood glue
Glue stick
Straight pin
Tape
Scissors
Utility cutter
Paper
Pencil

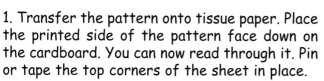

1. Transfer the pattern onto tissue paper. Place the printed side of the pattern face down on the cardboard. You can now read through it. Pin or tape the top corners of the sheet in place.

2. Carefully slit the plan along the marked line from point A to B.

3. Apply glue stick to the plan over cross-hatched area. Now, position the balsa wood fuselage (motor stick) on the plan.

5. Carefully cut two of the balsa strips to length to make the triangle fin. Carefully cut the correct angles to form a good fit.

6. Apply glue stick to the plan where the wood pieces will fit. Lay wood strips down accordingly. Apply wood glue at the three joints.

7. Cut out the fin, along the edges of the wood, starting at point A around to B.

8. Cut the wing frame pieces. Be sure to cut them at the correct, precise angles to fit perfectly to each other.

9. Frame the wing using the same method as the fin assembly (steps 5, 6, and 7). Glue each joint securely between pieces as indicated by arrows.

10. Construct the horizontal stabilizer portion of the tail in the same manner as the wings.

11. Cut the wing and horizontal stabilizer from the plan.

12. To balance your prop, hold the socket and carefully blow into the prop to make it turn. When it stops, if one blade points towards the ground it is the heavier blade. Scrape away

some plastic from the front of that blade until the prop balances from left to right.

13. Glue the wing to the fuselage. Pin in place. The leading (front) edge of the wing should be placed approximately 1 1/4" from the front edge of the fuselage. **Before glue dries**, turn over the Delta Dart. Hold in place on the cardboard and press the wings down carefully to form the dihedral angle.

14. Pin the wing to the cardboard so that the propeller and the rudder touch the board. Now apply extra glue at the joints where arrows point.

15. Glue the horizontal stabilizer (tail) to the rear of the fuselage. Make sure that it is at a 90 degree angle to the fin. **Let model dry for at least one hour.**

16. Carefully push in one pin at a slant near the front end of the tail to hold the rubber band motor in place.

17. Tie the rubber band motor to make a loop. The loop should be 8 1/2" long. Trim the ends to a length of 1/4". Suspend the rubber band motor from the propeller hook to the slanted pin. Position the knot at the motor back for smoother running.

18. Hold the fuselage with one hand under the wing. Wind the rubber band motor clockwise. Start with 50 turns for short test flights. If it flies correctly, increase the number of turns starting with 100.

19. Hold the propeller. Keep the nose of the Delta Dart in an upward attitude. Release the propeller as you launch the model with a gentle push. Your Delta Dart is now airborne.

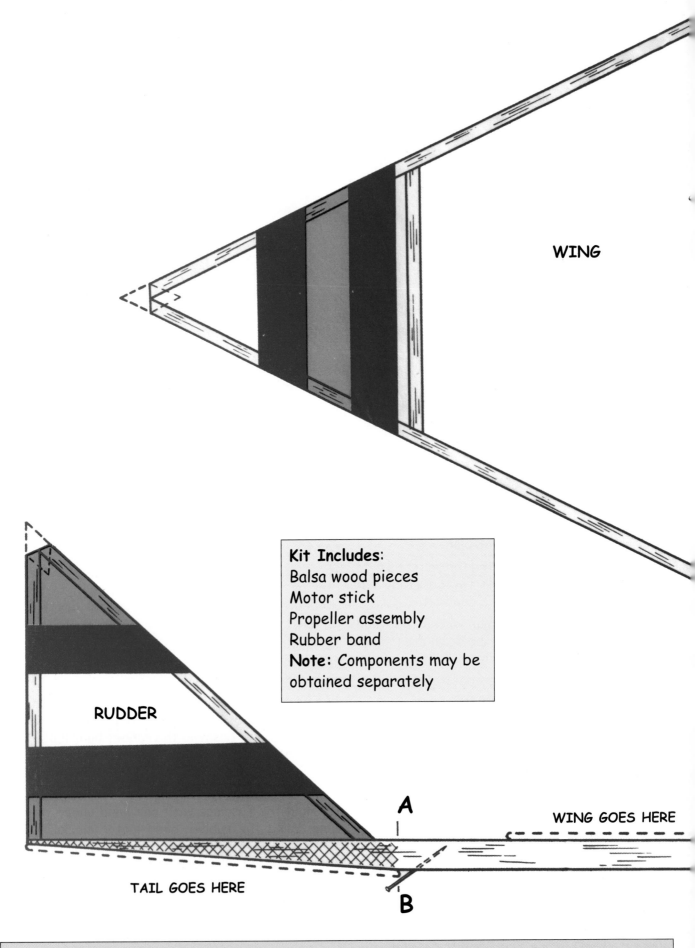

WING

Kit Includes:
Balsa wood pieces
Motor stick
Propeller assembly
Rubber band
Note: Components may be obtained separately

RUDDER

A

WING GOES HERE

TAIL GOES HERE

B

Midwest Products Co., Inc. Micro-Cut® Quality Woods Delta Dart; Fiskars® Scissors

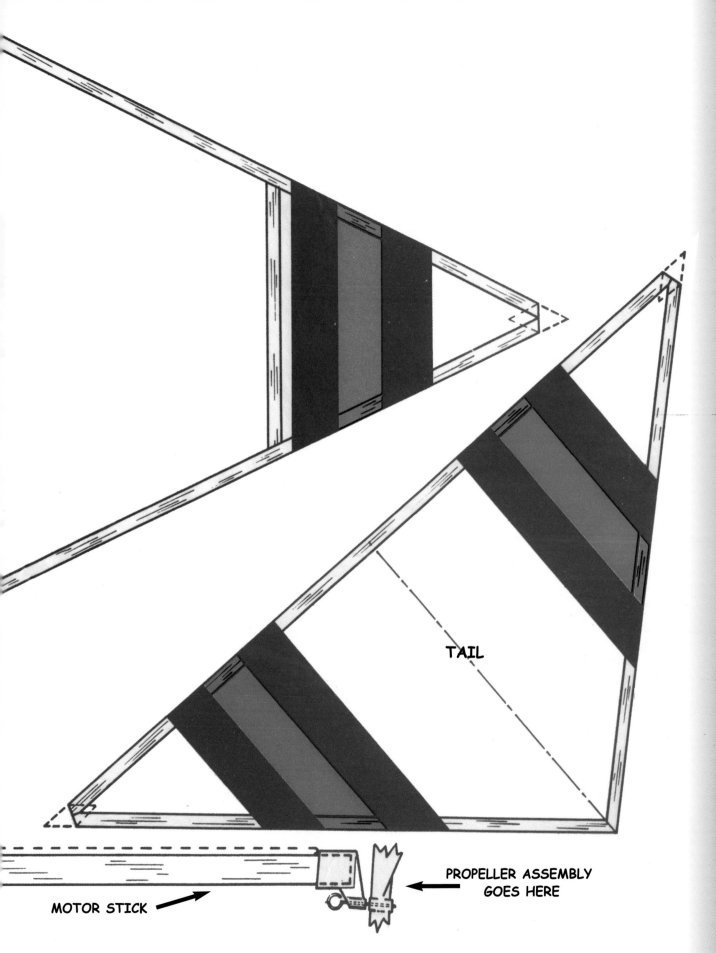

TAIL

PROPELLER ASSEMBLY
GOES HERE

MOTOR STICK

No matter where your journeys take you, you'll always be **Back In Time** to craft even more with these great products!